# Reading for Understanding

## Grades 3-4

By
**Elizabeth Flikkema**

**Cover Design by**
**Annette Hollister-Papp**

**Inside Illustrations by**
**Shauna Mooney Kawasaki**

*Publisher*
Carson-Dellosa Publishing Company, Inc.
Greensboro, North Carolina

# Credits

**Author:**
Elizabeth Flikkema

**Artist:**
Shauna Mooney Kawasaki

**Cover Design:**
Annette Hollister-Papp

**Cover Photograph:**
© Comstock, Inc.

**Project Director:**
Kelly Morris Huxmann

**Editors:**
Kelly Morris Huxmann, Karen Seberg

**Graphic Design:**
River Road Graphics

ISBN 0-88724-760-1

# Table of Contents

# Table of Contents (continued)

Name _____

# Science Experiment

What is air pressure? Can you feel the pressure of the air around you? This experiment will help you see and feel air pressure.

**Materials:**

wide-mouth jar or drinking glass
plastic sandwich bag or empty bread bag
thick rubber band

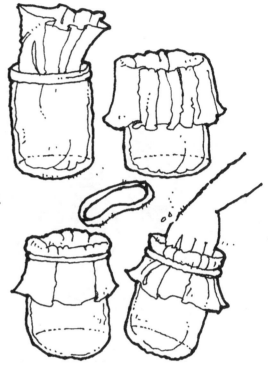

**Directions:**

1. Push a plastic bag deep into a jar.

2. Fold the rest of the bag over the edge of the jar.

3. Make an airtight seal with a thick rubber band.

4. Now try to pull the bag out of the jar.

**Answer the questions.**

**A.** Is it easy or difficult to pull the bag out of the jar?

_____

_____

**B.** What is keeping the bag in the jar?

_____

_____

**C.** What do you see? Draw a picture in the box.

Draw your picture here.

Cut out and staple the pages in order. Read about the planets in our solar system.

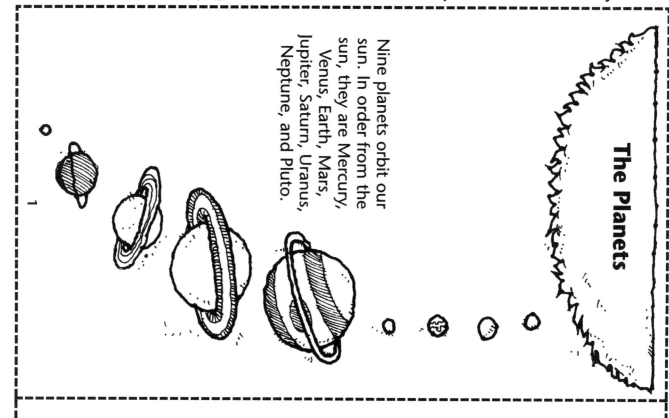

**The Planets**

Nine planets orbit our sun. In order from the sun, they are Mercury, Venus, Earth, Mars, Jupiter, Saturn, Uranus, Neptune, and Pluto.

1

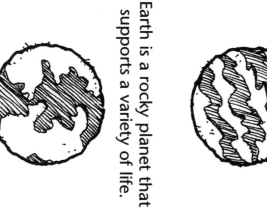

Mercury is the closest planet to the sun. It is the second smallest. It is a rocky planet.

Venus is the sixth largest and the hottest planet. It is often called Earth's "sister planet."

Earth is a rocky planet that supports a variety of life.

2

Uranus is a cold, gas planet.
Its surface is made of bits of rock and ice.
It looks pale green.

Neptune is a gas planet.
Sometimes it is the farthest from the sun.
It looks blue.

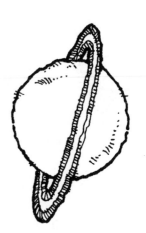

Pluto is usually the farthest from the sun.
It is the smallest and coldest planet.

4

Mars is a cold, rocky planet.
Its two poles are frozen with dry ice.

Jupiter is the largest planet. It is a gas planet.
The Great Red Spot on Jupiter is a storm.

Saturn is the second largest planet.
It is also a gas planet. It is known for its rings
that are made of ice and rock.

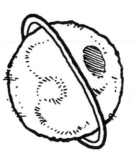

3

# What Is the Problem?

**Read each paragraph and answer the questions.**

Robbie and his dad were walking on the beach on a summer morning. They were talking about how beautiful the beach was. They were looking for signs of animals while the tide was low. Robbie saw something large up ahead on the beach. He and his dad ran toward it. It was a giant whale beached on the sand. Robbie's dad quickly ran to the nearest house so he could call the aquarium.

**1 a.** Who are the main characters in the story? _____

   **b.** What is the setting? _____

   **c.** What is the problem? _____

   **d.** How do you think the story will end? _____

_____

Marjie brought her new bike to Danielle's house. Danielle and Marjie took turns riding the new bike. They each rode it around the block several times. Marjie showed Danielle how she could ride her bike without holding the handlebars. Danielle wanted to try, too. Danielle got started and shouted, "Look, no hands!" Then Danielle fell on the sidewalk. She got up right away. Marjie asked if she was all right. Danielle said, "I'm fine, but I think your handlebars are twisted."

**2 a.** Who are the main characters in the story? _____

   **b.** What is the setting? _____

   **c.** What is the problem? _____

   **d.** How do you think the story will end? _____

_____

*Reading for Understanding*

 **Easy Dessert**

This dessert is so easy to make, you don't even need a spoon to stir it. The bars are best when cold so don't be too eager to taste them right out of the oven.

## Layered Bars

### Ingredients:

1 stick of butter
1½ cups (360 ml) graham cracker crumbs
1 cup (240 ml) nuts
1 cup (240 ml) chocolate chips
1⅓ cups (320 ml) coconut flakes
13 oz. (390 ml) can sweetened
   condensed milk

### Directions:

Preheat the oven to 325°F (165°C). Put a stick of butter in a 9" x 13" (23 x 33 cm) baking pan and place in the oven. Watch closely. Remove once the butter has melted. Pat the graham cracker crumbs evenly into the butter. Sprinkle the nuts over the crumbs. Then add the chocolate chips. Layer the coconut flakes over the chocolate chips. Pour condensed milk over the whole thing. Bake for 25 to 30 minutes. Let cool before cutting.

**Draw the steps for making layered bars. Label the steps and the ingredients.**

| | |
|---|---|
| **1** | **2** |
| **3** | **4** |

# Forest Animals

**Read the questions on the left and the answers on the right.
Draw a line from each question to its correct answer.**

| |
|---|
| Why do baby deer, or fawns, have spots on their backs when the adults do not? |

| |
|---|
| There is a strong odor right around the entrance. |

| |
|---|
| What causes a skunk to spray its perfume? |

| |
|---|
| It is awake at night when it hunts for mice and other small animals to eat. |

| |
|---|
| How can you tell when you are near a fox's den? |

| |
|---|
| The fawn's spots help it blend in with the colors of the forest and protect it from enemies. |

| |
|---|
| Why does a squirrel collect nuts in the fall and hide them in different places? |

| |
|---|
| They help take in sounds, so the animal hears very well. |

| |
|---|
| When does an owl do its hunting? |

| |
|---|
| When threatened by an enemy, it stamps its feet in warning, then turns around and sprays. |

| |
|---|
| Why does a rabbit have such long ears? |

| |
|---|
| The busy animal is storing food for the winter where other animals won't find it. |

# A Scary Story

Identify the story elements below.

**Story Elements**

| | | |
|---|---|---|
| when | what | where |
| | who | why | |

**3.** On the dark road home

_____

**1.** A 10-year-old boy

_____

**4.** Because he is alone

_____

**2.** Feels scared

_____

**5.** Late at night

_____

**Use the story elements above to write a scary story.**

_____

_____

_____

_____

_____

# Home Alone

**Read.**

Derrick shouted good-bye and waved to his friends as he ran up the front walk. He had come straight home from school today. He was eager to play his new computer game. Derrick turned the knob of the front door. It was locked!

Derrick's mom was always home from work before he got home. She worked at a bookstore and left each day at three o'clock. It was 3:45 and she still wasn't home.

Derrick was worried about his mom, but he decided to try to get in the house. He walked around the house and tried the side door. It was locked. The back door was locked, too. He thought a few minutes about climbing in through a window. Derrick thought his mom might be angry if he broke a screen or anything while trying to climb in the window.

Derrick felt his throat tighten and tears come to his eyes. He decided he wouldn't cry, and he wiped his eyes. "Think," he said to himself.

Just then, Derrick's neighbor drove up her driveway. He was so relieved. He ran right over to her. "My mom isn't home and I can't get in the house!" he shouted in one breath.

His neighbor said, "Come on in, Derrick. You can call your mom and wait here for her." Derrick followed Mrs. Phillips into the house. He sat at the kitchen counter. Mrs. Phillips gave him two cookies and a glass of water.

Derrick called the bookstore where his mom worked. Her boss said that she had left work on time. As Derrick hung up the phone, he felt his stomach tighten again. He wondered what could have happened to her. Derrick started to dial his grandma's phone number. At that moment, he saw his mom's car pull up in the driveway. He thanked Mrs. Phillips and ran out the door.

Derrick ran to his mom. She stepped out of the car and into his hug. "I'm so sorry," she said. "I was stuck in traffic on the highway. There was a terrible accident. My car didn't move for 20 minutes. All I could think about was you waiting for me. Are you okay?"

Derrick told his mother what he had done. And he said, "I wasn't worried for a minute."

# Home Alone (continued)

summarizing

**Read the story. Write your answers in complete sentences.**

1. Write a summary of what Derrick did when he came home from school. Leave out the details and just tell the main facts.

_____

_____

_____

_____

2. Write a summary of what you would do if the person who was supposed to pick you up from school didn't show up.

_____

_____

_____

_____

3. What are some safety rules to remember if you are home alone?

_____

_____

_____

_____

Name _____

# What's the Question?

Read the answers below. Before each answer, write an appropriate question. The first one has been done for you.

1. **Question:** _What are the names of three fairy-tale princesses?_

    **Answer:** Cinderella, Sleeping Beauty, and Snow White

2. **Question:** _____

    **Answer:** a tent, a sleeping bag, and a cooler full of food

3. **Question:** _____

    **Answer:** lettuce, broccoli, celery, and zucchini

4. **Question:** _____

    **Answer:** He was the first president of the United States.

5. **Question:** _____

    **Answer:** She was a black woman who refused to give up her seat on a bus and started the civil rights movement in the United States.

6. **Question:** _____

    **Answer:** It is a continent at the South Pole where penguins live, but no people call it home.

7. **Question:** _____

    **Answer:** You heat up milk on the stove and then add chocolate syrup and marshmallows.

8. **Question:** _____

    **Answer:** It is an animal with six legs, three body parts, and two antennae.

Name _____

**Read.**

Tristan took off his wet boots and sat on the couch. He looked out the window and smiled at the rounded figure in the yard. Tristan rubbed his hands together and blew on them. Ileana was in the kitchen making hot chocolate. He could hear her stirring the milk in the pan. He looked at the icy patterns on the window.

Ileana came in the room and handed Tristan his cup. "Hey, nice job out there!" she said. "That carrot makes a great nose! I hope your dad doesn't mind that we borrowed his scarf."

"Shall we read another chapter of your book before bed?" Ileana asked the yawning boy. Tristan moaned, "Do I have to go to bed so soon? Let's read two chapters."

"Your mom said you had to be in bed by 8:30 because you have school tomorrow," Ileana said. She found the book and started reading. Tristan listened to the story while he drank his hot chocolate.

**Circle yes or no.**

1. Ileana is Tristan's sister.    **yes**    **no**

2. It is winter.    **yes**    **no**

3. There is a person standing in the yard.    **yes**    **no**

4. Tristan has been playing outside.    **yes**    **no**

5. Tristan is probably around 18 years old.    **yes**    **no**

6. Tristan used the scarf and carrot to dress a snowman.    **yes**    **no**

7. Ileana is a baby-sitter.    **yes**    **no**

8. It is Saturday night.    **yes**    **no**

9. Tristan's mother is gone for the evening.    **yes**    **no**

**Draw a picture of Tristan and Ileana.**

# Saguaro Cactus

**Read.**

In the Arizona desert, a cactus grows that will live 100 years or more. The saguaro cactus grows very slowly in the hot dry desert, and it becomes home to many animals as it grows.

The cactus starts as a seed dropped from the fruit of a mature saguaro cactus. The seed sprouts after a rare rain gives it moisture. The seed swells up, splits its shell, and sends a root down into the desert soil. The seed sends up a stem that is green, moist, and covered with prickers.

It does not rain often in the desert, so the stem grows slowly. After one year, it has grown less than a centimeter. After 10 years, it may be only 15 centimeters (6 inches) tall. When it is 50 years old, the original stem is about 4½ meters (15 feet) high. After 50 years, the saguaro cactus grows its first branches. The branches are moist and prickly like the trunk. Over the next 50 years, the cactus may grow as tall as 10½ meters (35 feet) tall.

Many animals make their homes in the saguaro cactus. Animals like its moist skin. Woodpeckers may build a deep nest in the side of a saguaro stem and lay eggs there. After the eggs hatch, the baby birds eat insects that live on the cactus. Mice, hawks, and owls may also use the nest built by the woodpeckers.

Beautiful flowers grow on the mature saguaro cactus. The flowers provide juicy nectar for birds, insects, and bats that come to the cactus to drink.

After the flowers dry up, green fruits cover the cactus. The fruit is sweet and juicy. Many animals come to eat the fruit. They also spread the seeds from the fruit onto the ground where the seeds wait for rain. Eventually these seeds will sprout and grow new saguaro cactuses. The cycle goes on and on for hundreds of years.

# Saguaro Cactus (continued)

Draw the stages of the cactus life cycle. Label your pictures.
Choose a label from the word bank to write under each box.

| Word Bank | | | | | |
|---|---|---|---|---|---|
| 50 years | Flowers | Seed sprouts | Animal homes | Fruits | 100 years |

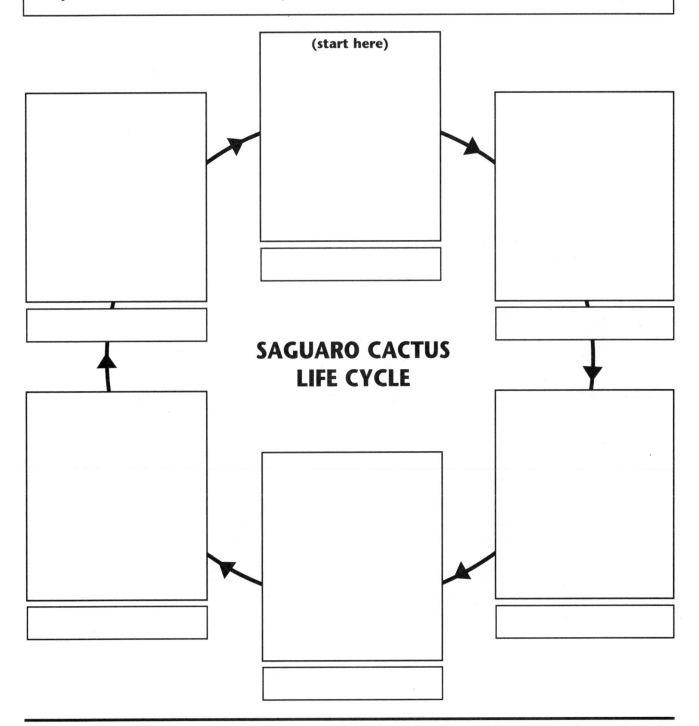

(start here)

**SAGUARO CACTUS
LIFE CYCLE**

# Skateboard

**Read.**

For his ninth birthday, Justin gets a new skateboard. He goes to the store with his dad and picks out all the parts for a custom-made skateboard. Justin picks out the wheels, the bearings, the trucks, and the deck.

Justin selects a deck first. The deck is the part of the skateboard you stand on. The bottom of his deck is red, yellow, and purple with a picture of a skull. Justin chooses rough, black grip tape to put on the top of the deck. The tape will give him good traction so his feet won't slip while he is doing tricks. Next he picks out blue trucks with yellow tabs. Justin decides to go with the smaller 54 mm wheels. He wants to be close to the ground on his skateboard. He chooses the bearings that are slow but not the slowest. He doesn't want the fast bearings, because even when standing still, the skateboard would slip around on the fast bearings. The guys at the store put the board together for Justin.

Back at home, Justin goes right outside to practice. Justin is not a brand-new skater. He has been using his brother's board for the whole summer. He knows how to ollie, which is to jump off the ground. With his new board, Justin likes to use the quarter pipe, a ramp used for doing tricks. He likes to "drop in" and "rock 'n' roll" on the quarter pipe. When he is a little more experienced, he may try a kick flip. To do a kick flip, he will have to kick the board in the air and land on it back on the ramp.

Justin and his brother also have a fun box. On the fun box, skateboarders can do lots of tricks. Justin tries to ollie on the fun box. He is starting to work on board sliding, too. He is still too new at it to try a 50-50 grind. His brother is teaching him how to do a finger flip. Justin grabs between the trucks, spins the board around, and tries to jump back onto it. It is hard to do.

Justin and his friends like to watch the older kids on their skateboards. Justin wants to be as good as they are someday. He learns by watching. He watches what they do well and he watches their mistakes.

Name _____

**Write your answers using information from the story.**

1. What does it mean that the skateboard is custom-made?

   _____

2. What part of a skateboard is the deck?

   _____

3. How does good traction help the skater?

   _____

4. Name three tricks that Justin can do.

   _____

5. Name four tricks that Justin would like to learn.

   _____

6. Name two places where Justin can try out his tricks.

   _____

7. List three ways that Justin will learn more about skateboarding.

   _____

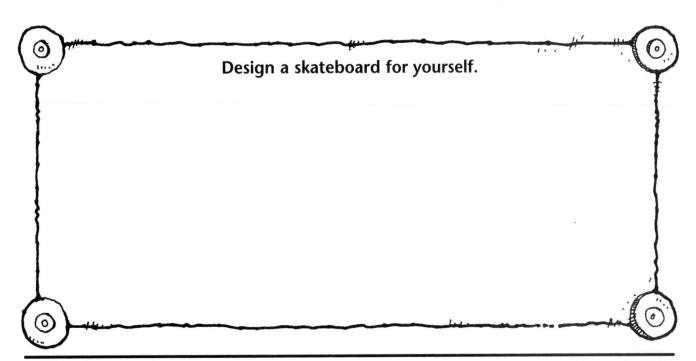

Design a skateboard for yourself.

Name _____

# What Have You Read?

Read the diagram. Then answer the questions.

## WHAT BOOK HAVE YOU READ?

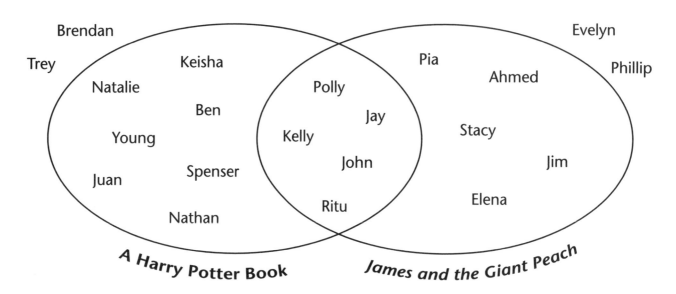

Brendan

Evelyn

Trey

Pia

Phillip

Keisha

Ahmed

Natalie

Polly

Ben

Jay

Stacy

Young

Kelly

Jim

Spenser

John

Juan

Elena

Nathan

Ritu

**A Harry Potter Book**

**James and the Giant Peach**

1. How many children have read a Harry Potter book? _____

2. How many children have not read a Harry Potter book? _____

3. How many children were questioned? _____

4. Which children have not read either book? _____

_____

5. How many children have read *James and the Giant Peach*? _____

6. Which children have read both books? _____

_____

Name _____

 # Helen Keller

**Read.**

Helen Keller was a well-known woman. She was born in 1880. When she was just 19 months old, she suffered a terrible illness that left her unable to speak, hear, or see. For several years after that, young Helen lived in utter darkness and silence. She was angry and afraid and acted wildly.

When Helen was seven years old, her teacher, Annie Sullivan, taught her to "hear" and "speak" with her hands. After that, Helen learned quickly. She even learned to use her voice, too. Helen went on to college and graduated with honors.

Helen was very smart and dedicated. She wrote books and gave many speeches. She worked hard to teach others about coping with disabilities. She also worked against unfairness and violence against people. Helen Keller lived to be 88 years old and became very famous.

**1.** List four of Helen Keller's greatest accomplishments (hard things she did).

_____     _____

_____     _____

**2.** Choose one of her accomplishments and write why it was hard for Helen.

_____

**3.** Write four words that describe Helen Keller.

_____          _____

**HELEN KELLER**

_____          _____

**4.** Imagine you could not see, hear, or talk. What would be different about your day? Tell about one change that you would have to make in the morning, the afternoon, and the evening.

Morning: _____

Afternoon: _____

Evening: _____

# Compost Pile

**Read.**

What happens to your garbage? Do you throw it all in the trash can? Not everything you throw away is trash. Some things can be recycled, some can be burned, and some can be composted. A compost pile is a pile of leaves, grass, and some leftover foods that you keep outside.

It is not difficult to make a compost pile. All you need is a small corner of your yard to make a pile. Some people keep their compost in a large wooden box that doesn't have a top. Other people buy special bins that turn the compost for you. You fill the compost mostly with shredded newspaper, grass, and leaves. People also put their apple peelings, eggshells, and vegetable ends in the compost pile.

You have to take care of your compost pile. If you don't stir it, it can really start to stink. The compost also needs some sunshine and water. If you take care of your compost, the pile will not get any bigger even if you keep adding things to it. A compost pile works in two ways: the sun and water help the leaves, grass, and food leftovers to rot; and little red worms eat the garbage. As the worms eat the compost materials, their bodies turn the food into rich soil. You can use that soil to make your garden grow better. Composted soil works just like a fertilizer.

A compost pile helps you in lots of ways. You will have less garbage to throw away each week. That means garbage dumps will fill up more slowly. It may also mean you pay less money for garbage collection. A compost pile can make very good natural fertilizer for your yard, garden, or houseplants. A compost pile is a fun science experiment, too. You will be amazed by how quickly the pile gets smaller and by how many critters will live there.

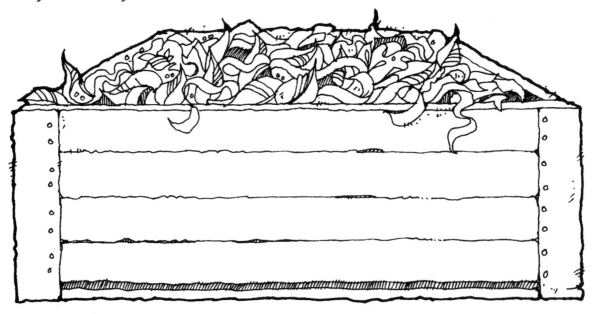

# Compost Pile (continued)

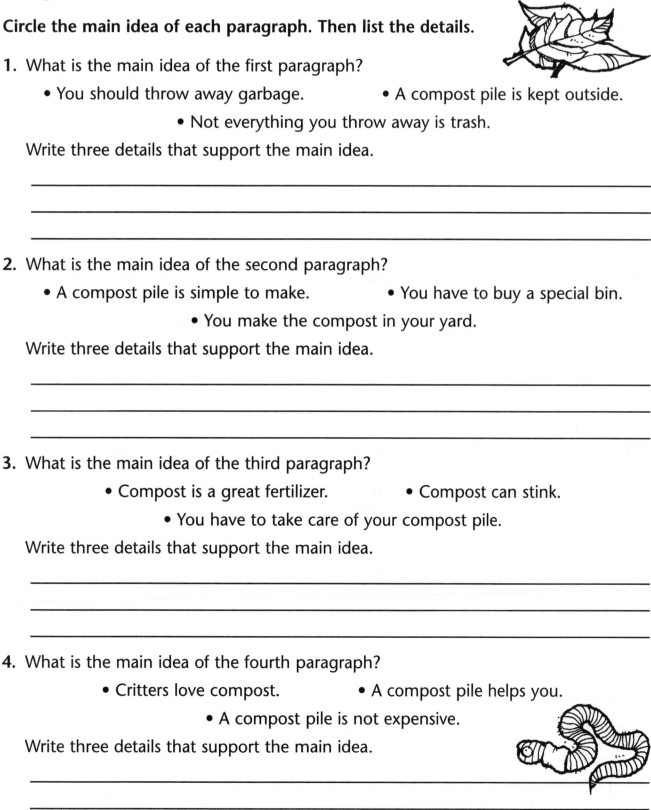

**Circle the main idea of each paragraph. Then list the details.**

1. What is the main idea of the first paragraph?

   • You should throw away garbage.          • A compost pile is kept outside.

   • Not everything you throw away is trash.

   Write three details that support the main idea.

   _____

   _____

   _____

2. What is the main idea of the second paragraph?

   • A compost pile is simple to make.          • You have to buy a special bin.

   • You make the compost in your yard.

   Write three details that support the main idea.

   _____

   _____

   _____

3. What is the main idea of the third paragraph?

   • Compost is a great fertilizer.          • Compost can stink.

   • You have to take care of your compost pile.

   Write three details that support the main idea.

   _____

   _____

   _____

4. What is the main idea of the fourth paragraph?

   • Critters love compost.          • A compost pile helps you.

   • A compost pile is not expensive.

   Write three details that support the main idea.

   _____

   _____

# Whales

**Read.**

There are many different kinds of whales. Whales are not fish; they are mammals. They swim in the water, but they breathe air. A whale breathes through the blowhole on the top of its head. It has smooth skin that allows it to move quickly in the water. Whales use their strong tails to push themselves forward. They have a thick layer of blubber under their skin that keeps them warm. There are two main groups of whales: toothed whales and baleen whales.

Toothed whales have teeth and eat fish, squid, and other sea animals. Baleen whales do not have teeth. Instead, they have a baleen which they use to strain their food. The baleen is made up of hard, comb-like plates that hang down from the whale's upper jaw. When it wants to eat, the baleen whale swims through the water with its mouth open. When it closes its mouth, the water rushes out and the tiny animals are trapped inside.

Blue whales are one type of baleen whale. Blue whales are not only the largest whales, they are also the largest animals that have ever lived. A blue whale can grow to be nearly 30 meters (100 feet) long. The blue whale's tongue alone can weigh as much as an elephant.

The blue whale likes to eat krill, which is a tiny shrimp. Krill live in cold water so blue whales spend their summers near the North and South Poles. They spend their winters in warmer water where there is less krill. When there isn't much krill, they need to live off the blubber they have stored up in their bodies.

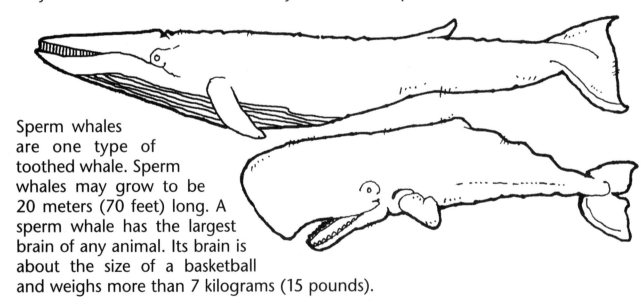

Sperm whales are one type of toothed whale. Sperm whales may grow to be 20 meters (70 feet) long. A sperm whale has the largest brain of any animal. Its brain is about the size of a basketball and weighs more than 7 kilograms (15 pounds).

# Whales (continued)

The sperm whale is strong and powerful and likes to eat squid. Squid are tough animals. The whale needs to fight the squid in order to eat it. Sperm whales live all over the world, but they usually stay away from the coldest waters near the North and South Poles. The sperm whale has a large head that is filled with a waxy substance called spermaceti. The spermaceti may help the whale float.

For hundreds of years, people have hunted whales. They have hunted them for their meat and blubber. Hunters have sold the parts of the whale for money. The blue whale's baleen was once sold to make jewelry. The sperm whale's spermaceti was sold to make candles and make-up. Some whales were becoming endangered because of the hunting. Now, whale hunting is against the law in most countries.

**Complete the Venn diagram to compare blue whales and sperm whales.**

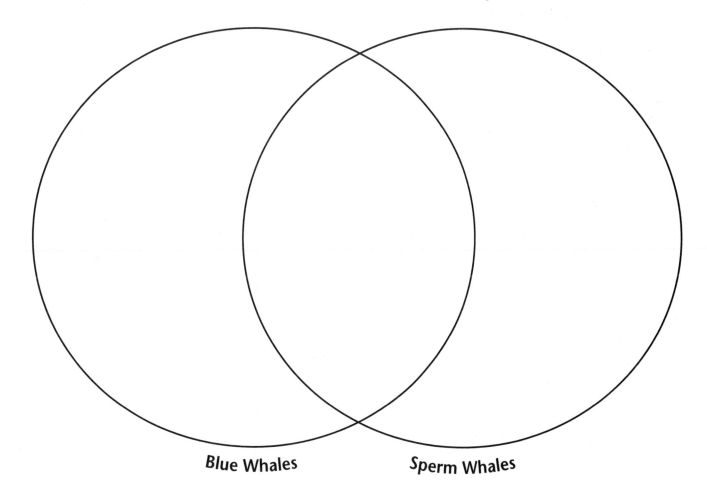

Blue Whales          Sperm Whales

# Make a Pop-up Book

following directions

Do you like to write? Maybe you like to write stories or poems for other people to read. Do you like to make your own greeting cards? If you would like to make your cards or written stories look a little flashier, try a pop-up book. The directions are easy if you follow them carefully.

1. To make one page, you will need two pieces of paper. Fold both pieces in half.

   **Step 1**

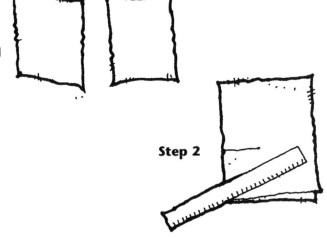

2. Make a pop-up tab in one sheet of the folded paper. Use a ruler to measure and draw two lines from the center of the folded edge. The lines should be 2 cm apart and 4 cm long.

   **Step 2**

3. Cut along the lines and fold the tab back and forth to make a firm fold.

   **Step 3**

4. Open the page and push the tab from the fold to the inside.

   **Step 4**

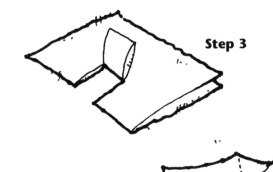

5. Close the page and press flat. Then open the page to see the pop-up tab.

   **Step 5**

# Make a Pop-up Book (continued)

**6.** Glue the page with the pop-up tab on top of the other sheet of folded paper. Do not put glue on the tab.

Step 6

**7.** Draw, color, and cut out a picture to glue onto the pop-up tab. The picture should be bigger than the tab but not so big that it sticks out when the page is folded in half.

Step 7

**8.** Glue the picture to the tab.

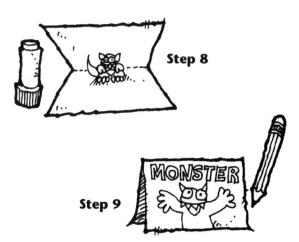

Step 8

**9.** Decorate the outside of the page and write the story on the inside.

Step 9

## Other Ideas

**A.** Make more than one pop-up on a page.

**B.** Make pop-ups in different shapes and sizes.

**C.** Put several pop-up pages together to make a pop-up book. Use a glue stick rather than liquid glue for a neater look.

A

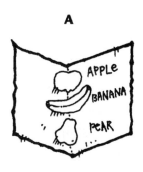

B

C

 # Dinosaurs

**Circle fact or fantasy after each statement. Then read the article about dinosaurs.**

1. Dinosaurs were all huge and terrifying.      **fact**    **fantasy**

2. Dinosaurs are all extinct.      **fact**    **fantasy**

3. Dinosaurs lived here where we live today.      **fact**    **fantasy**

4. Dinosaurs were green and brown.      **fact**    **fantasy**

5. All dinosaurs ate other dinosaurs.      **fact**    **fantasy**

6. Cave people protected themselves from dinosaurs with clubs.      **fact**    **fantasy**

7. Scientists can figure out what sounds the dinosaurs made.      **fact**    **fantasy**

The most exciting thing about dinosaurs is that they are gone. They lived on the same earth as us for 160 million years, but now they are extinct.

No human ever saw a living dinosaur. The first dinosaurs lived over 225 million years ago. The first dinosaurs were probably extinct long before the tyrannosaurs or triceratops showed up. Then 65 million years ago, the last dinosaurs could no longer be found walking on earth. It is exciting to imagine how life looked then right here where we are sitting today. Since we only have their bones to learn from, we must take the pieces we have and imagine the rest.

Paleontologists are scientists who study fossil remains like dinosaur bones and the rocks that surround them. They look for clues that tell how dinosaurs looked and acted. They compare what they find with what they know about animals living today. They act like detectives to learn more about these mysterious animals.

Scientists now know that there were many kinds of dinosaurs and they were all different from each other. Some ate meat and others ate plants. Some were large and some were small. Some took care of their young, while others left their young to grow up on their own. The only thing scientists will never know for sure is what color the dinosaurs were.

Imagine how exciting it must be to dig up an old skeleton. From the bones, scientists may discover what the dinosaur ate, how it stood and moved, and where it lived. They may even figure out what sound it made! They can learn all of this even though people never saw living dinosaurs!

# Dinosaurs (continued)

**After you've read the article, look at these statements again. Circle fact or fantasy. Did any of your answers change?**

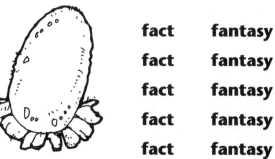

1. Dinosaurs were all huge and terrifying.                    **fact**    **fantasy**

2. Dinosaurs are all extinct.                                 **fact**    **fantasy**

3. Dinosaurs lived here where we live today.                  **fact**    **fantasy**

4. Dinosaurs were green and brown.                            **fact**    **fantasy**

5. All dinosaurs ate other dinosaurs.                         **fact**    **fantasy**

6. Cave people protected themselves from dinosaurs with clubs.  **fact**    **fantasy**

7. Scientists can figure out what sounds the dinosaurs made.   **fact**    **fantasy**

**Draw a picture of a dinosaur based on the following description.**

The dinosaur stood about as tall as a mature oak tree. It walked on its hind legs. It used its front legs for balance and fighting. The dinosaur had sharp teeth for tearing. It had a small head with a curved tube that ran from its nose over its head. The tube was used for making sounds. The dinosaur's long tail helped it balance. The sharp points on its tail could be used in an attack.

**Compare your drawing with your classmates' drawings. Do all of your pictures look the same? What differences do you notice?**

_____

_____

_____

# Lemonade Stand

**Read.**

Faiza and Emily set up a small wooden table at the corner of Cambridge and Sherman Streets. Faiza wiped the table and set up the supplies. Emily set up two chairs and a large umbrella that shaded the table and chairs. Soon they would be open for business.

The girls painted a sign. They lettered the sign carefully: "Lemonade for Sale." They colored the words bright yellow and outlined them in black. They leaned the sign in front of the table.

Then the girls went inside and came back with a heavy cooler. Inside were two pitchers of ice-cold lemonade and a bag of ice. They also had a container of homemade cookies.

They took one pitcher out of the cooler and set it on the table. Then they put 10 cookies on a plate and covered them with plastic wrap. They sat down in their chairs and waited.

A car drove by. It didn't stop. A few minutes later, another car drove past. Emily yelled, "Lemonade for sale! Twenty-five cents a cup!"

The car kept driving. A third car came by and parked at the neighbor's house. Faiza and Emily both shouted, "Lemonade for sale! Twenty-five cents a cup!" Faiza's neighbor stepped out of the car and waved at the girls. She walked over to the lemonade stand.

"Hi, Mrs. Ford," said Emily. "Would you like some lemonade?"

"Sure," said Mrs. Ford. She gave the girls a quarter and drank her cold lemonade. "Are those cookies for sale, too?" asked Mrs. Ford. She bought two cookies and said good-bye.

Emily and Faiza stayed at their lemonade stand for two hours. Many people walked by and bought lemonade and cookies. By the time they ran out of lemonade and cookies, they had earned six dollars.

# Lemonade Stand (continued)

sequencing

**Put the events of the day in order by numbering the sentences from 1 to 10.**

_____ They carried out the heavy cooler.

_____ Emily set up the chairs.

_____ The neighbor bought some lemonade.

_____ The girls set up the table.

_____ They put 10 cookies on a plate.

_____ They put one pitcher of lemonade on the table.

_____ The girls stayed at the lemonade stand for two hours.

_____ They earned six dollars.

_____ They painted the sign.

_____ Two cars drove by without stopping.

**Imagine that Emily and Faiza wanted to tell their neighbors that they were going to have a lemonade stand again the following Saturday. Design an advertisement that they can take to their neighbors' houses letting them know about the lemonade stand. Be sure to include all the important information (who, what, where, when, and how much).**

Cut out and staple the pages in order. Read about how maple syrup is made.

1

MAKING MAPLE SUGAR

2

Long ago, Native Americans used their tomahawks to tap maple trees for sap. They boiled the sap in clay pots to make maple sugar.

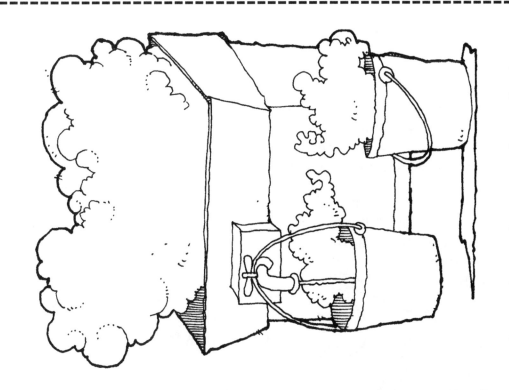

The sap is mostly water. After collection, the sap is boiled in a "sugar shack" or sugarhouse, a house with a large stove in it. When the water is evaporated out at just the right temperature, pure maple syrup is left.

4

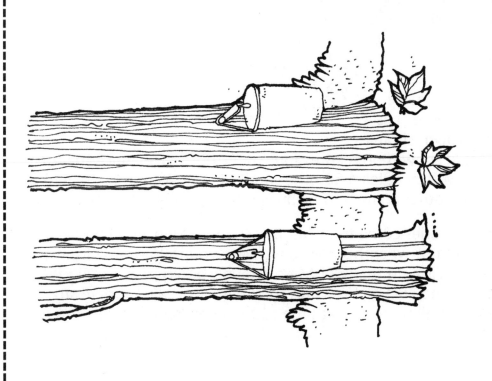

Maple trees produce a sweet sap that can be tapped in early spring. The maple syrup producers bore holes in the trees that are 5 cm deep and 1 cm in diameter.

They drive a spout into each hole and direct the sap into a bucket or a series of tubes.

3

# Marc Brown

**Read.**

Marc Brown is the best-selling author of the Arthur books. You may have read *Arthur's Nose, D.W. Thinks Big*, or *Arthur and the True Francine*. These books and others tell about the life of an aardvark, his family, and his quirky animal friends.

Marc Brown loves drawing and telling stories. He had a wonderful grandma (Grandma Thora) who told stories. Mr. Brown got his love of telling stories from her. He told many stories to his own boys, who are now grown-ups. He especially loved to tell animal stories. One day he told a story about an aardvark named Arthur. That was how the Arthur stories were born.

From the time he was six years old, Marc Brown has enjoyed drawing. His wonderful Grandma Thora loved his drawings. She saved his drawings and told him to draw more. He knew he must have been pretty good because his grandma didn't usually save things. Marc Brown draws the pictures for all of the Arthur books and writes the stories.

Arthur has been around for many years. The first Arthur book was published in 1976. That book was called *Arthur's Nose*. In that book, Arthur had a long nose like a real aardvark. In the more recent books, Arthur's nose has gotten smaller. Mr. Brown shrank Arthur's nose so he could show more expressions on Arthur's face. Since that first book, Marc Brown has written at least 30 other books about Arthur, D.W., Binky, Francine, Buster, and the other animals in Arthur's school and neighborhood.

The ideas for the Arthur stories come from Mr. Brown's experiences when he was a child. They also come from when his own boys were young and now from life with his young daughter Eliza. In many of Marc Brown's books, you can find the names of his sons, Tolon and Tucker. He writes their names on packages in stores, on jackets, and in other small places. Next time you read an Arthur book, look for their names.

# Marc Brown (continued)

**Answer the questions in complete sentences.**

1. What does Marc Brown love to do?

   _____

   _____

2. How do you think Marc Brown felt about his grandma?

   _____

   _____

3. How do you think Marc Brown feels about children?

   _____

   _____

4. If you could ask Marc Brown one question, what would you ask?

   _____

   _____

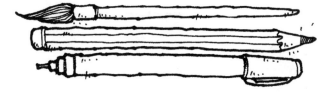

**Circle the best answers.**

A. What is Marc Brown like?

   • funny      • sad      • unfriendly      • rude      • creative      • bored

B. Which of these sentences would Marc Brown say?

   • I wish children would stop writing me letters about Arthur and the gang.

   • Imagine how exciting it is to use a pencil or computer and your imagination
     to create whole new worlds and new ideas.

   • I don't have enough time to do the things I really love to do.

# Paper Towels

**Read.**

Do you know that many inventions were accidents? Sometimes new ideas come to people when they are working on something else. Paper towels were invented because of a mistake. The Scott Paper Company made the first paper towels. They weren't out looking for a better towel. The paper towel just showed up at their factory one day.

The Scott Paper Company made toilet paper. They ordered the fine tissue in long rolls from a paper mill. Then they cut the rolls into the right size and packaged them for home use.

Unfortunately, one day a shipment came from the paper mill that was all wrong. The tissue was too thick and wrinkled. The buyers were ready to send the ruined paper back, when someone had an idea. He said that the thick paper would make nice hand towels that people could use and then throw away.

The Scott Paper Company perforated the rolls of thick paper so they would tear into towel-sized pieces. They packaged the paper rolls and sold them in stores as "Sani-Towels."

Instead of sending the mistake back, Scott Paper Company created a new product that still sells well over 100 years later. So you see, mistakes can be a great learning experience if you can think in a new way.

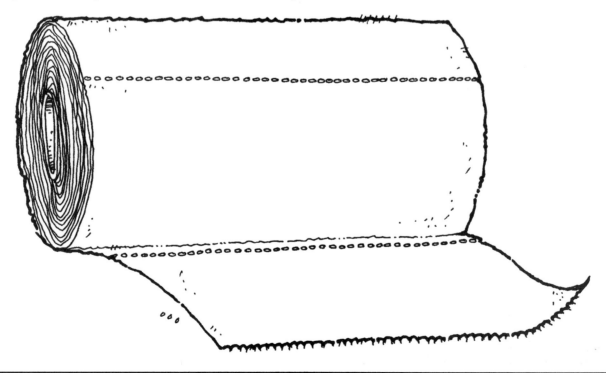

Name _____

# Paper Towels (continued)

**Sometimes opinions get in the way of new ideas. Try to look at just the facts. Cross out all the opinions.**

"I'm sorry to tell you, Mr. Scott,
that we have an incorrect shipment of paper from the paper mill."

"The paper is bad."

"This paper is thick and wrinkled."

"Tissue paper is thin and smooth."

"Thick paper is too tough."

"Wrinkled paper is ugly."

"This is thick enough to be a hand towel."

"Hand towels should be washable."

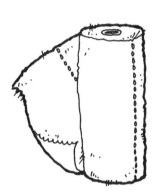

**Something that one person throws away may be a great discovery for someone else. What could you make with these throwaway items?**

1. _____

2. _____

3. _____

4. _____

Name _____

# Penny's New Glasses

**Read.**

Penny had a hard time seeing the board in class. Rosa sat next to her. Penny asked Rosa to read her the assignment each day. One day, their teacher said, "Penny, I think you should go to the eye doctor."

Penny's mom made an appointment, and, in a few weeks, Penny was waiting in the office of the optometrist. The optometrist called her name and she went into a darkened room. On one side of the room was a large chair with a robot-looking machine in front of it. The doctor told her to sit in the chair. The doctor sat on a small stool on rollers and introduced herself. "I'm Dr. Riley."

Dr. Riley pulled the machine over to Penny. Part of the machine looked like a mask. Dr. Riley told Penny to look through the mask and read some letters on the opposite wall. As Dr. Riley turned some dials, the letters became blurry and then clear. Dr. Riley kept turning dials until Penny said that the letters were very clear and easy to read.

When Dr. Riley was done, she brought Penny to another room where the optician helped her pick out frames for her new glasses. Penny picked out small, round frames that were black. The optician told Penny that her glasses would be ready in about a week. Penny wished she could wear her new glasses home. She was excited.

In a week, Penny went back and picked up her new glasses. She liked the way she looked with her glasses. Her mom said she looked smart.

The next day at school, Penny wore her new glasses. She couldn't wait to show her friends. "It's about time you got glasses," Rosa said. "I'm tired of reading the board for you." Penny laughed when Rosa smiled. Penny was surprised to hear someone call her "four eyes."

During math, Penny could read the problems on the board. In reading, she had no trouble reading her book. In gym class, Penny made a basket. She felt great about how clear everything was now. The next time she heard someone say "four eyes," Penny said, "The better to see you with, my dear." Penny and her friends laughed so hard at that, they almost cried.

**38**

# Penny's New Glasses (continued)

**Answer the questions in complete sentences.**

1. Why did Penny's teacher think Penny should go to the eye doctor?

   _____

2. How did the eye doctor know how strong Penny's glasses should be?

   _____

3. What does an optometrist do?

   _____

4. What does an optician do?

   _____

5. Did Penny like wearing her new glasses?

   _____

6. How did Penny feel when someone called her "four eyes"?

   _____

7. List three things Penny could do better when she wore her glasses.

   _____

   _____

   _____

8. What did Penny do when someone teased her about her glasses?
   Circle your answer.

   • She cried.

   • She told a joke.

   • She stopped wearing her glasses.

   • She told the teacher.

**Draw a picture of yourself with glasses.
Draw the shape and color of the frames
you would like to have if you were able
to get new glasses.**

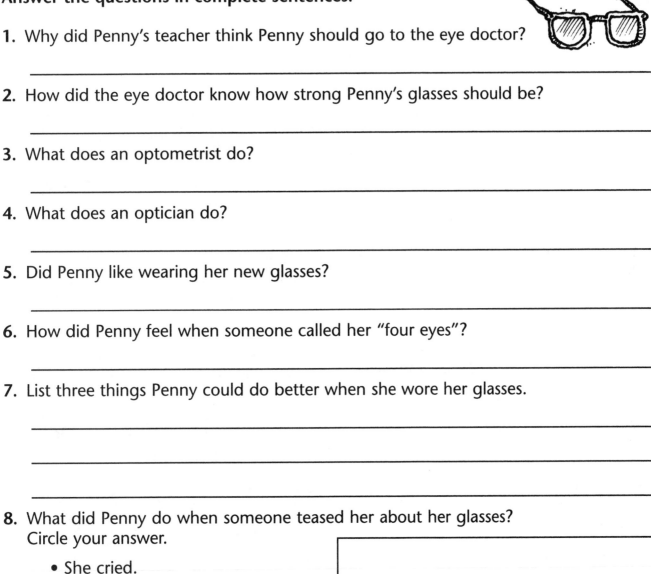

# Peterson's Pockets

**Read.**

I love pockets! When I pick out a new coat each year, I look for the coat with the most pockets. I especially like hidden pockets. I once had a coat with 12 pockets! I loved that coat.

I also love pants with lots of pockets. I love those pants that have pockets on the side of the leg. I like to put things in my pockets. I put money, bottle caps, cool stones, my yo-yo, notes from my friends, and other stuff I find in my pockets.

My mom doesn't like it that I put stuff in my pockets. Sometimes I forget to take papers out of my pockets before my mom washes my pants. She says it makes an awful mess in the washing machine.

My dad said that long, long ago, pants didn't have any pockets at all! Back then, people wore little pouches that hung from their belts. I would have had to wear a pretty big pouch. My mom says I would have to carry around a suitcase if I didn't have all these pockets.

Did you know that the first pockets on pants were little pouches sewn on the outside of the pants? About 200 years ago, pockets finally were sewn on the inside of pants like they are now.

Someday, I'm going to invent a new place to hide a pocket. Maybe in 200 years, people will be talking about me and my super cool pocket. They will wonder how people ever got along without the "Peterson pocket."

Name _____

# Peterson's Pockets (continued)

point of view

This story was written from the point of view of Peterson, a boy who loves pockets. Write the same story from the point of view of either his mother or his father.

_____

_____

_____

_____

_____

_____

_____

_____

_____

_____

Think of a new place to hide a pocket. Then draw your design. Use labels to describe where the pocket is and what it could hold.

# Recycling

**Read.**

All across the country, garbage trucks are picking up trash at every house and bringing it to the town dump. The piles of trash at the dumps are getting bigger and bigger. We are running out of places to put our trash. But we have ways of reusing some of the things we used to throw away. In addition to the garbage truck, the recycling truck now comes to many houses to pick up recyclables.

The recycling truck is made just for picking up recyclables at your house. There are separate bins in the truck for paper, cardboard, glass, and cans. When the truck comes to your house, the driver separates the materials you left at the curb into the right bins. The truck goes to the recycling center instead of the dump.

At the recycling center, the driver dumps the glass bottles into a big dumpster. The bottles break as they fall into the container, but that is okay. The bottles will be sold to a company that melts the glass and makes new bottles.

The driver dumps the cans into a big machine. The machine has magnets in it. These magnets separate the steel cans from the aluminum cans. The cans are then crushed and sent to companies that melt the cans and use the metal again.

Paper and cardboard are loaded into a machine that crushes them and ties them up in bundles. These bundles are sold to paper companies that process the old paper to make fresh paper and cardboard.

There are two good reasons to recycle. First, if we all recycle everything we can, garbage dumps will not fill up as quickly. Second, recycling and reusing old materials means we use up fewer new materials. This is all good news for the health of our planet.

# Recycling (continued)

## Answer the questions.

1. What items belong in each bin? Write the letter of the correct bin next to each item.

GLASS    METAL    PAPER    CARDBOARD    PLASTIC    TRASH

**A**     **B**     **C**     **D**     **E**     **F**

_____ empty soup can

_____ glass soda bottle

_____ mayonnaise jar

_____ used facial tissue

_____ newspaper

_____ cottage cheese container

_____ envelopes

_____ junk mail

_____ pop can

_____ shampoo bottle

_____ crushed box

_____ broken toy

2. What happens to each material? Draw a line to show what happens to each material.

glass bottles        processed and made into new material

broken toys        melted and made into new material

junk mail        crushed, melted, and made into new material

pop cans        thrown in a garbage dump

3. What are two reasons to recycle?

_____

_____

4. Do you recycle at home?_____

5. Do you recycle at school? _____

# Shortcut

**Read.**

We probably should have taken the road home from the baseball park. It was getting dark, though, and we decided to take the shortcut home. I was the oldest and should have made a better choice. I didn't know there would be a train.

The shortcut from the baseball park to home was along the train tracks. After Reggie's game was over, we were excited. The game had gone into overtime and Reggie's team had won! As we walked, Reggie and I gave each other high fives. Samantha and little Brittany were running to keep up while they chewed on their candy necklaces. You know how little sisters are. When we came to the turn for the shortcut, we were so excited and happy that we just took it. We should have stayed on the road.

We walked for about five minutes on the tracks. The sides of the tracks were steep and there were thick bushes and marshy water at the bottom. We stayed on the tracks. Samantha asked how we'd know if a train was coming. I said that we'd feel the tracks rumbling.

It was then that I heard the train whistle far away. You never can tell when a train will come through. I didn't want to worry the little ones, so I just said as calmly as I could, "Let's go back to the road." We turned around and I walked pretty fast. Everyone followed.

Soon we felt the tracks rumbling and I shouted, "Run!" I grabbed little Brittany in my arms and Reggie held Samantha's hand. We ran as fast as we could. Then I could see the headlights and the train blew its loud whistle. We kept running, but I shouted, "Get off the track, NOW!" We jumped off the tracks. We all slid down the sides, trying hard to keep out of the scratchy bushes. Samantha and Brittany were crying but I could not hear them. The loud train was rushing by us.

After the train went by, we climbed back up the hill. We were all scratched up from the bushes, but no one complained. We were all shaking as we walked back to the road. It was dark. We didn't have to talk. We all knew we'd never take the shortcut home again.

# Shortcut (continued)

drawing conclusions

**Answer the questions in complete sentences.**

1. What bad choice did the children make?

_____

2. In what way were the children brave?

_____

3. In what way were the children careless?

_____

4. Do you think all the children knew they were in
   danger when the train whistle blew the first time?     **yes       no**

   Why do you think that? _____

   _____

5. Why were the children shaking as they walked back to the road?

   _____

6. Do you think they will ever take the shortcut home again?     **yes       no**

   Why do you think that? _____

   _____

7. Why didn't the children complain about the scratches from the bushes?

   _____

   _____

Name _____

# The Doll Store

**As you read the following story, you will be asked some questions. Answer the questions before you read ahead in the story.**

Madeline loved to sew. One day, she found lots of tan fabric in her mom's fabric box. She asked her mom if she could use it to make a doll. Her mom said yes.

Madeline cut a doll shape out of the tan fabric. She cut a second shape exactly like the first one, sewed them together, and stuffed the doll full of pillow stuffing. Madeline found two brown buttons that she sewed on the doll's face for eyes. She drew on a mouth with red fabric paint. Then she made some hair with black yarn. Madeline measured her new doll and sewed her a simple flowered dress. Her doll looked great! Madeline named the doll Hazel.

Madeline took her new doll to her room and played with it for a while. As she was playing, she had a thought. "I bet all my friends would like to have a doll like Hazel," she said to herself. "They'd probably even pay to buy one." Madeline had an idea. "I wonder if Mom would let me use more of that fabric…"

**1.** *What do you think Madeline will do next?* _____

_____

Madeline went to her mother and asked if she could use the rest of the fabric. When her mother said yes, Madeline squealed with delight. She decided to make enough dolls for all of her friends in the neighborhood. Madeline spent the next few days making dolls. Each doll had the same body but different eyes, hair, and clothes. She gave each doll a name. Finally, she thought she had enough dolls to set up a store in her front yard.

Her mom helped her put a small table and chair in the front yard. Madeline made a sign that said, "Dolls for sale! $5 each." Madeline put her eight new dolls on the table. She put a card by each doll with its name on it. Then she sat and waited.

**2.** *What do you think will happen next?* _____

_____

**3.** *Will Madeline sell any of her dolls?* _____

# The Doll Store (continued)

predicting outcomes

It wasn't too long before her neighbor Holly came over to see what Madeline had. Holly looked at all the dolls and said that she would like to buy Tina, the doll with the red dress. She asked Madeline to hold the doll for her while she went home to get her money. Madeline held the doll in her arms and watched Holly run home. She realized that she did not want to sell Tina. Madeline hugged Tina and tried to decide which doll Holly would like just as much as Tina. But Madeline loved all of her dolls! How could she sell any of them?

**4.** *How does Madeline feel about her dolls?* _____

_____

**5.** *What do you think she will do?* _____

_____

When Holly returned, Madeline was still sitting at the table hugging the doll. Holly could tell something was wrong by the look on Madeline's face. "What's wrong, Madeline?" Holly asked. "Are you okay?"

Madeline told Holly how she felt. Holly understood, but she still wanted the doll. Holly said, "Let me help you pack up your table and dolls. We can play with the dolls together for a while. Then maybe I can still buy the doll and we can play together anytime you want." Madeline agreed and the girls played.

At dinnertime, Madeline let Holly take the doll home, but she didn't sell it to her. She would let Holly play with Tina for a while, but she would still be Madeline's doll. Maybe she would set up her doll store again tomorrow. She just didn't know yet.

**6.** *What do you think Madeline will do tomorrow?* _____

_____

**7.** *Write an ending to the story.* _____

_____

_____

_____

_____

# The Fort

**Read.**

All the kids in the neighborhood loved to play in the fort. The fort was a small fenced-in area behind the empty house on the corner. The house had been empty and for sale for six months. Every day the kids played in the fort. Nobody could see them there. They played cops and robbers; they held court; they pretended they had a school. Then one day someone bought the house.

The fort was a place that was no good for anything but a fort. One side was made of the back of the garage. The second side was the back of the deck. The third side was the side of the neighbor's garage. The fourth side was the back fence of the house on the next street. To get to the fort, the kids had to walk between the side of the garage and the neighbor's fence. When the "Sold" sign went up on the house, the kids all wondered what would happen to their fort.

A new family moved into the house. They had little kids. That was promising. They were friendly people, but who would ask them about using the fort? Day after day, the fort was empty. The neighborhood kids played in the front yards together, but all they talked about was the fort. They missed playing there, but they stayed away all summer.

When the kids went back to school in the fall, they talked about the fort again. "I think we should ask the new neighbors if we can play there," said Alex. The kids agreed and sent Alex and Brian to go knock on the door. When the door opened, Alex nervously asked, "May we play in the fort behind your house? We used to play there and we will be careful."

"Well, I don't know," said the new owner, Mrs. Johnson. "Let's go back there together and you can show me what you are going to do there. Then we can talk about whether you may play there."

The neighbor kids showed Mrs. Johnson the fort. They showed her how they got in and where they played. When they were done explaining, Mrs. Johnson said, "Okay. You may play here if you promise to play safely and pretty quietly."

That sounded fair to everyone, so they agreed. Now the neighborhood kids meet at the fort after school. They play cops and robbers, school, and court. They take good care of the fort and play quietly. Once in a while, they have little visitors from the Johnson house. The kids invite the little ones in and they have a tea party. Mrs. Johnson supplies the tea and cookies.

**Answer the questions in complete sentences.**

1. What is the effect of the house being sold?

   _____

2. What causes the neighborhood kids to stay away from the fort?

   _____

3. What is the effect of the new neighbors moving into the house?

   _____

4. What causes the kids to knock on the Johnsons' door?

   _____

5. What is the effect of knocking on the Johnsons' door?

   _____

6. What rules does Mrs. Johnson set in effect?

   _____

7. What is the cause for the kids having a tea party?

   _____

   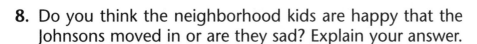

8. Do you think the neighborhood kids are happy that the Johnsons moved in or are they sad? Explain your answer.

   _____

   _____

   _____

# What's in an Egg?

**Read.**

Everyone knows that chickens come from eggs, but did you know that many other animals also come from eggs? Animals that make eggs that hatch outside their bodies are "oviparous." Eggs come in all sizes from microscopic to large dinosaur eggs. Some eggs need to be in the water and some eggs stay on land.

Many animals that live in the water produce eggs. Eggs in the water are usually soft-shelled. Fish lay eggs in the water. Some fish eggs are heavy and sink to the bottom of the lake or ocean. Other fish eggs are light and float in the water. The male seahorse carries eggs in a pouch in his belly. The female octopus lays her eggs in long strands that she hangs from the roof of an underwater cave. The American oyster can release up to one hundred million eggs at a time. Frogs lay their eggs in clumps. Toads lay eggs in strands as long as 15 feet (14½ meters).

Other animals lay their eggs on dry land. These eggs usually have hard shells and contain food for the growing baby inside. Most birds lay their eggs in nests made from twigs and grasses. A nest helps the mother keep her eggs safe and warm. Some birds use mud and sticks in their nests. Others use moss and bark. Some tiny hummingbirds use spiderwebs in their nests. Some female penguins lay their eggs and give them to the fathers to keep warm. The father penguin can stand on the ice with the egg on his feet for eight weeks!

Insects lay eggs, too. Many insects lay their eggs in a sac. They may attach the sac to a leaf or branch. Most insects are on their own as soon as they are born. Spiders wrap their eggs carefully in silk thread and carry them with them or put them in a safe place.

Almost all mammals carry their babies inside their bodies until they are born alive. There are only three species of mammals that lay eggs: the duck-billed platypus, the short-nosed echidna, and the long-nosed echidna.

Eggs can come in many sizes, colors, and textures. A fertilized egg contains the start of a new life and carries hope for the animal to bring more of its kind into the world.

Name _____

Fill in the chart with information from the article.

| ANIMAL | DESCRIPTION OF EGG | LOCATION OF EGG |
|---|---|---|
|  |  |  |
|  |  |  |
|  |  |  |
|  |  |  |
|  |  |  |
|  |  |  |
|  |  |  |
|  |  |  |
|  |  |  |
|  |  |  |

Draw and decorate an invented egg. Show where it would hatch and how it would stay well camouflaged and protected. Describe the animal that laid the egg.

# A Day at the Beach

**Read.**

Erika and Yesenia rode together in the backseat. They were excited because they were going to the beach. Erika had never been to the beach before. She was going with her best friend Yesenia's family.

Yesenia told Erika all about the sand and the waves. She told her about the paddle boat. "I like to paddle out to the deep part and jump in the water," said Yesenia. Erika felt her stomach tighten. She didn't know how to swim. She didn't know that Yesenia was so brave in the water. Erika didn't say anything.

At the beach, the girls had a great time. They played in the water, jumping in the waves and laughing. They built a huge sand castle using buckets and shovels. They let water in and created a moat. Erika thought the beach was great!

Then Yesenia's dad called them over to the boat dock. He had the paddle boat ready for them and held two life jackets in his hands. Yesenia ran to the boat, put on her life jacket, and sat down. She smiled and waited for Erika. Erika was very nervous. Yesenia's dad helped her put on her life jacket. Erika carefully climbed into the seat and put her feet on the pedals. Yesenia started pedaling so Erika did too. Soon they were moving quickly across the water. It was fun. When they were far out in the lake, Yesenia stopped the boat and said, "Last one in the lake has stinky feet!" Yesenia jumped in the water. Erika didn't move. She didn't dare tell Yesenia that she couldn't swim. Would Yesenia laugh at her?

Yesenia watched Erika. Finally she said, "Are you coming in?" When Erika shrugged her shoulders, Yesenia guessed what was wrong. She climbed back in the boat. "Do you know how to swim yet?" she asked kindly. Erika shook her head. Yesenia smiled at her friend and said, "Okay. Let's paddle around some more. Then after lunch, I'll teach you a little bit about swimming." Erika smiled at her best friend. Why had she ever worried about telling Yesenia that she didn't know how to swim?

 # A Day at the Beach (continued)

**Answer the questions in complete sentences.**

1. What do you think Yesenia would have done if Erika had told her right away that she couldn't swim?

   _____

2. Why do you think Erika waited to tell Yesenia that she couldn't swim?

   _____

3. Why do you think Erika didn't know how to swim?

   _____

4. How do you think Erika can learn how to swim?

   _____

5. What did the girls have fun doing at the beach?

   _____

6. Do you think Yesenia will invite Erika to the beach again? Why or why not?

   _____

7. Do you think Erika will go to the beach again if she is invited? Why or why not?

   _____

**You can tell a lot about people by what they say and how they act.
Circle the best answers.**

**A.** What is Erika like?

| • bossy | • quiet | • cautious | • selfish | • doesn't listen |
| • a worrier | • brave | • nervous | • unafraid | • a bad friend |

**B.** What is Yesenia like?

| • bossy | • helpful | • brave | • caring | • doesn't listen |
| • cautious | • kind | • nervous | • selfish | • a good friend |

Name _____

**Read the questions on the left and the answers on the right.**
**Draw a line from each question to its correct answer.**

| | |
|---|---|
| In what year did the *Niña*, the *Pinta*, and the *Santa María* set sail to find a better route to India? | He left from Spain in 1492. |
| From what country did Christopher Columbus set sail? | They brought smallpox, a disease never seen on the island before. |
| What disease did Christopher Columbus's group bring to the island? | The ships sailed in 1492, but they landed in the West Indies, not India. |
| What good news did Columbus bring back to Queen Isabella? | They brought enough food for one year, including cheese, olive oil, dried beans, raisins, salted meats, rice, and honey. |
| How many days were the ships at sea before they saw land? | They were at sea for more than 30 days. The sailors were beginning to think the world was flat. |
| What food did they bring along on the journey? | He told her of the new land that Europeans did not know about before. |

Name _____

 # Campfire Walking Salad

Before you pick up your hot dog at the campfire, make a walking salad. You won't need a fork or plate for this salad. Just wrap the salad fixings in a piece of lettuce and carry it in one hand.

**Ingredients:**

large lettuce leaves
mayonnaise
peanut butter
salted Spanish peanuts
raisins
miniature marshmallows
raw carrot shavings

**Directions:**

Wash and pat dry several leaves of Bibb or leaf lettuce. Set out the ingredients on a table. Choose a lettuce leaf and spread mayonnaise or peanut butter on it. Then add other toppings. Roll up the lettuce like a tortilla and eat.

**Draw the steps for making a walking salad.
Label the steps and the ingredients.**

| 1 | 2 |
|---|---|
| 3 | 4 |

# A Family Hike

**Read.**

We started on the trail early in the morning. The sun was rising in the sky and the air around us was cold and misty. The pine trees looked like arrows pointing our way to the top of the mountain. It was a wonderful morning.

My mom and dad each carried a heavy backpack full of food, tents, water, and other things. Ben and I carried packs, too. Mine only had my clothes and sleeping bag in it. I carried a few snacks in my pockets and two water bottles on my belt. Ben is bigger than I am so he carried some food and a cookstove in his pack.

We walked quietly at first. My dad says you don't need words to be part of the forest in the morning. I could hear birds singing and chipmunks moving through the leaves on the ground. There was no breeze so the trees were silent. We walked single file along the trail.

At lunchtime, we stopped by a stream that flowed down the mountain. We could see a small waterfall higher up, but here the water cut through the rock and snaked past flowers and bushes. We took off our shoes and dipped our feet in the water. The sun shone brightly overhead and we all took off our jackets.

I knew better than to ask how much farther we had to go. My parents always say that our destination is the hike itself. We would be walking for three days on these trails. We would see many beautiful sights and hear and smell things we don't hear or smell at home in the city. My mom and dad are teachers. Every summer, we take a trip as a family. Ben wanted to bring a teenage friend, but my dad said that this was family time. Ben complained, but I know he likes family trips, too.

At dinnertime, we stopped and set up our tents on a flat meadow. We could see the next mountain peak from our site. It looked beautiful as the sun set behind it. We lit a fire and cooked dinner. We stayed awake a while longer to watch the stars. My mom pointed out several constellations. I want to be an astronomer someday.

We went to bed pretty early because we were all tired from walking. Tomorrow, we will have another long walk. We will reach the top of the mountain tomorrow. I have never stood on a mountaintop before. My dad says that I will be able to see forever. I think I'll like that. Maybe I will be able to see my friend Gena's house back home. I will wave to her and shout hello. I'll hear the echo and pretend that she shouted back at me. But that is tomorrow, and my dad says that even the night is part of the journey. So I will close my eyes and listen for the owls, the wind in the trees, and the sound of my dad snoring. I love this place!

**Answer the questions.**

1. Do you think that there is anyone else in the family who is not on the hike? Explain your answer.

   _____

   _____

2. How old do you think Ben is?_____

3. Do you know if the narrator is a boy or a girl?_____

4. Do you think the narrator likes this trip? _____
   Underline the sentences in the story that make you think that.

5. Where is the family hiking? _____

6. What time of year do you think it is? _____

7. Do you think that this family has been on a hike before? Explain your answer.

   _____

8. What senses does the narrator use while hiking? _____

   Give examples of what the narrator experiences with each sense. _____

   _____

**Circle the phrases that the parents might say on this trip.**

- We'll be there in one hour.
- Turn up the music.
- Don't rush.
- Getting there is half the fun.
- I don't have all day!
- Listen, did you hear that?
- Next time, you can stay home.
- Take one step at a time.

Name _____

# Animal Diagram

**Look at the Venn diagram. Then answer the questions.**

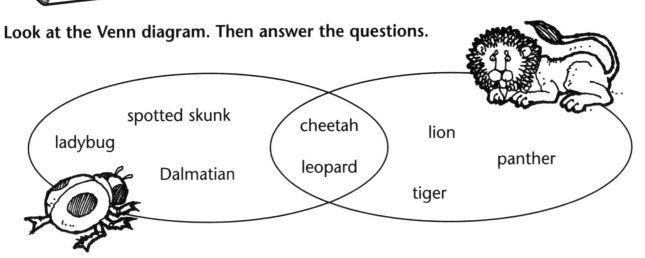

ladybug

spotted skunk

Dalmatian

cheetah

leopard

lion

panther

tiger

1. What is true of all the things in the first (left) circle, including the intersection?

   _____

2. What is true of all the things in the second (right) circle, including the intersection?

   _____

3. What would be a good title for this diagram?

   _____

4. How would you label each section of the diagram?

   **Circle 1:** _____

   **Circle 2:** _____

**Draw a Venn diagram with the following headings and fill it with details.**

   **Circle 1:** nocturnal animals

   **Circle 2:** birds

# Advertisement

**Look at the advertisement. Then answer the questions.**

## YOU NEED A SNUGGLE PET.

Shouldn't everyone experience the joy of having a pet? You will love your Snuggle Pet even more because you never have to feed it or bathe it. It snuggles with you. It comes when you call. Your Snuggle Pet even does tricks. Choose your favorite: Snuggle Pets come in monkeys, dogs, cats, and birds. It's worth the joy at any price!

(Prices may vary. Some assembly required.
Cost of clothes, pet toys, routine maintenance, and batteries not included.)

1. What is this advertisement trying to sell you? _____

2. What technique does the ad use to convince you to buy this toy?

    • It will make life easier.        • It will save you money.

        • Everyone should have one.

3. What does the advertisement tell you is good about the toy?

    _____

    _____

4. What does the advertisement tell you is bad about the toy?

    _____

5. What should you be careful about when buying this toy?

    _____

    _____

# Chewing Gum

**Read.**

My name is Thomas Adams. You probably have no idea who I am, but I invented chewing gum. Well, *invented* might be a strong word.

I lived in the 1800s. I once met General Santa Anna. He was a Mexican general. Santa Anna told me about a dried sap called chicle. He liked to chew this sap that came from the sapodilla tree. He said that Mayans and others had been chewing it for hundreds of years. I tried some. Honestly, I thought it tasted terrible.

Still, I was interested in chicle because it was so rubbery. I thought maybe I could make things like toys or boots out of it. But nothing I tried seemed to work. It just wasn't going to replace rubber.

One day, I popped a terrible-tasting piece of chicle in my mouth and chewed and chewed. Yuck, I thought. Wouldn't it be nice if it had some flavor? Eureka! I had a great idea! I opened a flavored-gum factory and sold chewing gum like crazy.

Americans loved my gum. But doctors seemed to think it was bad. They said it was bad for your teeth. Well, that may be true, but one doctor even said, "Chewing gum will exhaust the salivary glands and cause intestines to stick together." Isn't that the silliest thing you have ever heard?

I am proud to say that flavored chewing gum was a hit! But why doesn't anyone know my name?

 Chewing Gum (continued)

**Circle the best answers.**

1. How does the author feel about chicle?

   • friendly    • curious    • disgusted    • angry

2. How does the author feel about flavored chewing gum?

   • embarrassed    • worried    • proud    • curious

3. What did the author think the chicle could do?

   • replace gum    • become rubber    • replace rubber    • ruin teeth

4. What did the author think about what one doctor said?

   • He was right.    • He was silly.    • He was late.    • He was smart.

**Write in complete sentences.**

A. Why does the author think people should know his name?

_____

B. Write a brief summary of this story from your own point of view.

_____

_____

_____

C. Write a brief summary of this story from the point of view of the doctor who did not think that gum was safe.

_____

_____

_____

_____

# Don't Bug Me!

**Read.**

Have you ever had a mosquito bite? If you were bitten by a mosquito, that mosquito was a female. Only female mosquitoes bite. They need your blood to feed their eggs. Male mosquitoes just eat plant juices. Females eat plant juices, too, but they also need blood in their diets.

Animal blood and human blood contain protein. Mosquito eggs need that protein in order to be healthy and hatch. When the mosquito has gathered enough blood, she is ready to lay her eggs. So when she bites you, she is ensuring that there are more mosquitoes born.

When a mosquito bites, she is actually poking your skin with her stinger. Your blood normally starts to thicken, or clot, as soon as it leaves your body—this is an important part of healing. However, a tiny mosquito does not want the blood she sucks to clot in her stinger, or proboscis, so she spits a chemical while she bites. The chemical in her saliva keeps your blood from clotting in her proboscis. This chemical is what makes a mosquito bite feel itchy. Most people are allergic to this chemical. Their bodies react to the chemical by swelling, getting red, and itching. Some people itch more because they are more sensitive to the chemical.

Female mosquitoes are pretty annoying. They whine in our ears and take our blood. Then they leave behind an itchy reminder wherever they bite. If you don't like to itch, remember the bug spray next time you go out.

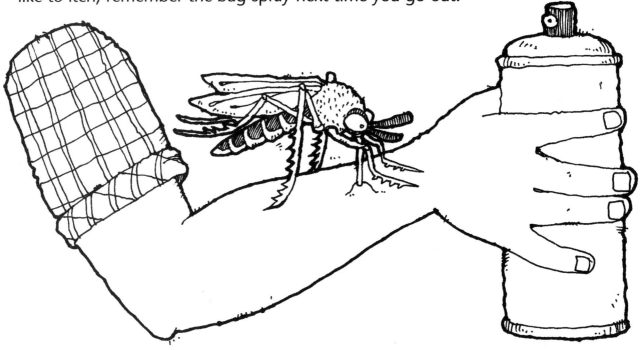

# Don't Bug Me! (continued)

**Fill in the blanks with words from the article that make sense.**

1. If you were bitten by a mosquito, that mosquito was a _____.

2. The mosquito needs your _____ to feed her _____.

3. Mosquitoes also _____ plant juices.

4. Both animal and _____ blood contain protein.

5. When the mosquito has enough blood, she is ready to _____.

6. Blood starts to _____ as soon as it leaves our bodies.

7. A mosquito doesn't want blood to clot in her _____.

8. Mosquitoes spit a _____ while biting.

9. The chemical makes a mosquito bite feel _____.

10. Our body reacts to the chemical by _____.

11. Mosquitoes _____ in our ears.

12. If you don't like to itch, remember the _____ next time you go out.

**Write an acrostic poem about a mosquito. Write a word related to mosquitoes vertically on the page. Then write a phrase or word that begins with each letter.**

*Example:*

**Title:** _____

**Splat**

_____

**S** Swat that mosquito,

_____

**P** Please!

_____

**L** Let's not

_____

**A** Allow her to

_____

**T** Take my blood again.

_____

_____

 **Insects**

**Read.**

Insects are truly amazing animals. They come in beautiful colors and a variety of interesting shapes. Insects are just about everywhere! They live in cold and hot climates. They live in wet jungles and dry deserts. They can live underground and high in the trees. There are at least one million different species of insects, and every year, new species are discovered.

Insects do many of the same things we do but in unique ways. Insects can hear, but some insects hear with hairs that cover their bodies. Other insects have hearing organs on their legs. Some insects hear from the sides of their bodies. Some insects smell with their antennae. Others taste with their feet.

Some insects are beneficial to humans. Bees make honey. Bees, wasps, butterflies, and other insects pollinate flowers and other plants. Some fruits and vegetables would not produce seeds without insects. Some insects eat or destroy pests that ruin our crops. Insects are also an important part of many animals' diets. Birds, fish, and frogs eat insects. Some insects even taste good to people!

Some insects are harmful to humans. There are insects that eat our crops. Some insects get into our homes and destroy clothes, books, and stored foods. Termites can be serious pests when they chew the wood frames of buildings! Worst of all, some insects carry diseases that can make people sick or die.

Although all insects have six legs, three body parts, and two antennae, each species of insects looks and acts uniquely. Insects can be beautiful or ugly, helpful or harmful, noisy or quiet. With all that variety, insects help make the world a very interesting place.

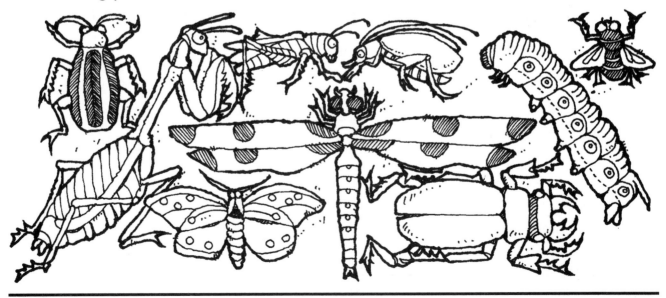

# Insects (continued)

**Circle the best answers.**

1. What is the main idea of the article?

   • Insects are beautiful.     • Insects are dangerous.     • Insects are interesting.

2. What is the main idea of the second paragraph?

   • Insects hear with their legs.     • Insects taste with their feet.

   • Insects' sense organs are in different parts of the body than in humans.

3. What is the main idea of the third paragraph?

   • Insects eat pests.     • Insects can be helpful.     • Some people like insects.

4. What is the main idea of the fourth paragraph?

   • Insects are dangerous.     • Insects eat wood.     • Insects can be harmful.

5. What is the main idea of the fifth paragraph?

   • Insects are beautiful.     • Insects can be harmful.

   • Insects make the world more interesting.

**Draw a picture of the last insect you saw.**

Where did you see it?  What was it doing?  Was the insect helping in some way?
Was the insect causing harm?

# Managing Fires

**Read.**

Firefighters have a difficult but important job. They are highly trained and brave people who put out fires. They work hard to save people from getting hurt in a fire. They also try to prevent personal property from being damaged. But there are some fires that firefighters do not try to put out.

In 1972, a new policy was written. It said that if a fire is started by lightning in a national forest or park, it should not be put out unless it causes a threat to buildings, personal property, or the logging industry. Now firefighters must also decide if a fire should be left to burn or not.

Fire is a natural part of the life cycle of a forest. About every 300 years, a natural fire can clean up a mature forest that is overgrown with underbrush and crowded with fallen trees. The fire can burn up the mess and make room for healthy new growth. These natural fires usually burn themselves out on their own.

When there is a natural fire, firefighters watch it burn very carefully. They make sure that the fire does not get out of control. A strong wind can make a natural fire grow too large and threaten areas where people work or live.

Some forest fires are not started naturally. A careless person might throw down a burning cigarette and start a fire. Other careless campers may let a campfire get out of control. If one of these fires starts in the forest, the firefighters will immediately work to put out the fire.

When firefighters must put out a large fire in a forest, they use many different methods. Firefighters use hoses and water from local lakes and streams to try and stop the flames. They may use axes to cut away trees that could burn and spread the fire. In some cases, they use bulldozers to push burnable materials away from the fire. Sometimes airplanes drop chemicals over the fire. These chemicals slow down the fire. Another method is to light "backfires." A backfire is a small, controlled fire that burns up the fuel (trees and shrubs) of a huge forest fire. Firefighters try to remove the materials that feed the fire so that the fire will stop.

All uncontrolled fires are dangerous. What a relief it is to know that we have brave, trained firefighters to keep fires under control!

# Managing Fires (continued)

drawing conclusions

**Answer the questions in complete sentences.**

1. What skills should a firefighter have?

   _____

   _____

2. When should a fire be left to burn?

   _____

   _____

3. What is a controlled fire?

   _____

   _____

4. Why would firefighters light a fire in order to put out a forest fire?

   _____

   _____

5. What does it mean to be brave?

   _____

   _____

6. What does a firefighter watch for when allowing a forest fire to burn naturally?

   _____

   _____

7. How can a fire be good for a forest?

   _____

   _____

8. What does it mean to be careless?

   _____

   _____

# Paul Bunyan

**Read.**

Paul Bunyan was a large boy born in the logging woods of Maine. He grew to be big and strong, but Paul remained a peaceful and kind person. Paul's family business was logging. His father cut down trees and sold them to lumber companies.

Paul was so strong that he could cut down five trees with just one swing of his axe. His father soon grew rich with all the trees that Paul cut down. The family sold their home in the small town and bought a large area of wilderness in the backwoods of Maine.

In the backwoods, Paul became friends with the wild animals. He wrestled with the bears and ran with the deer. One day, Paul was out walking in a snowstorm that left four feet of blue snow on the ground. He stumbled over a cold, shivering, blue ox calf. Paul hugged the animal, warmed him up, and took him home. Paul named the ox Babe. They were friends for life.

When Paul was old enough to leave home, he packed up a bag and set off with Babe to see the West. Paul cleared trees as he went and made a path for the pioneers to follow when they moved west.

Paul's first big job was to dig a shipping channel so he could send the logs he cut back to Maine on boats. He spent one day digging out the Great Lakes and the St. Lawrence Seaway. He hired a crew of men to help him clear the Great Plains of trees. After that big job, Paul Bunyan was tired. He let his axe drag behind him and he carved out the Grand Canyon.

It is said that Paul Bunyan and Babe made it to the West Coast and then traveled around the country some more. Stories tell that Paul still lives in the wilderness. He is caring for the animals and trees that need his help.

Name _____

 **Paul Bunyan (continued)**

**Write your answers in complete sentences.**

**1.** Paul Bunyan was a large man, but stories exaggerate his size and strength. Write down five exaggerations from the story.

_____

_____

_____

_____

_____

**2.** Write two exaggerations of your own for Paul Bunyan. Make sure your exaggerations fit where and when he lived.

Size: _____

Strength: _____

**3.** Write an exaggeration about something you did or about one of your personal characteristics.

_____

_____

_____

_____

Name _____

# The Giant Sequoia

**Read.**

Far out west in the California sun grow some giant trees that have been around for millions of years. The first giant sequoia trees probably started growing about 180 million years ago. They were probably around when dinosaurs walked the earth. Now the heat-loving trees only grow naturally in California.

Giant sequoias can live for more than 3,000 years. For the first 250 years, giant sequoias look like small pine trees. When they are about 500 years old, they reach their full height. The giant sequoia can grow as tall as a 25-story building—that's about 76 meters (250 feet) tall! Some trees have grown up to 9 meters (30 feet) wide—that's as wide as a three-lane highway! The largest giant sequoia living today is named General Sherman. General Sherman is over 83 meters (274 feet) tall.

There are not many sequoias around anymore. Millions of years ago, sequoias grew all over North America, but then the weather turned colder. These trees love the warm weather. Now when people visit sequoia forests, they drive and walk all over the ground. This makes the ground hard. The roots have a hard time soaking up water in the hard ground. This is killing some of the precious trees. Some people take home seeds when they visit the sequoia forests. They plant the seeds all over the world. Someday these small trees may develop into new forests.

A forest fire is actually good for a sequoia forest. The fire burns the small trees that grow in the shade of the giant trees. This allows the small sequoia seedlings to grow better, because they get more sunlight and water. Before the fire, they had to share that sun and water with the other trees. Also, the heat from a forest fire opens up the cones that grow high up in the trees. The seeds locked in the cones flutter down to the ground and start new trees.

When a huge sequoia tree dies, it falls onto the forest floor. There it continues to contribute to the life of the forest. Many animals build their homes in the fallen tree. As the tree decays, it becomes fertilizer for other plants. The cycle of life found in the giant sequoia forests is amazing to see.

# The Giant Sequoia (continued)

**Answer the questions.**

**1.** How long have sequoia trees been growing in North America?

_____

**2.** How long does it take for a giant sequoia to reach its full height?

_____

**3.** How tall is the tallest sequoia tree?

_____

**4.** About how many years can a sequoia tree live?

_____

**5.** Why is a forest fire good for the sequoia forest?

_____

**6.** What are two reasons that sequoias are not around as much anymore?

_____

**7.** How do sequoia trees take in water?

_____

**8.** What do sequoias need in order to survive?

_____

**9.** How does a dead sequoia help the forest?

_____

# Taking Care of Teeth

**Read.**

Long ago, people cleaned their teeth in some pretty interesting ways. They may have scratched their teeth with a stick, wiped them with a rag, or even chewed on crushed bones or shells. Tooth care has come a long way in the past few hundred years. Now we have fluoride toothpaste, dental floss, and specially angled toothbrushes to keep our teeth healthy.

It took someone with a lot of time on his hands to invent the first toothbrush. In the 1770s, a man named William Addis was in prison. While he was sitting around wiping his teeth with a rag, he had the idea to make a tool for cleaning teeth. He used a bone and some bristles from a hairbrush. He carefully drilled holes in one end of the bone. Then he trimmed some bristles from a brush and pushed them into the holes he had made. He glued the bristles in place.

People have used different tooth cleaners over the years. Many cleaners, such as crushed bones or shells, actually damaged the protective enamel on teeth. Chalk was a popular cleaner in the 1850s. Baking soda was used for many years as well, because it was an abrasive. Some toothpastes still contain baking soda. Other people used salt as a tooth cleaner. Many of today's toothpastes contain sodium, too. Fluoride was first added to toothpaste in 1956 and greatly reduced the number of cavities in children. In the 1980s, calcium was added to toothpaste to help strengthen teeth.

Using dental floss once a day is one of the most important things you can do for your teeth. The thin string was originally made of silk. Now dental floss comes in colors, flavors, tape, and waxed and unwaxed varieties. Dental floss removes "interproximal plaque accumulation." This means that it scrapes the plaque off between your teeth where a toothbrush cannot reach.

The inventions and improvements in dental care have meant that people are growing up with stronger, healthier teeth. We now know what foods are bad for our teeth and how to care for our teeth every day.

Name _____

**Circle your answers.**

**1.** What is the author's purpose in writing this article?

• to entertain        • to teach        • to sell something

**2.** What kind of article is "Taking Care of Teeth"?

• a factual article        • a humorous article        • a fictional article

**3.** What is the main idea of the article?

• how to take care of teeth        • the importance of flossing

• the history of dental care

**Complete the web to demonstrate what you learned.**

**Why use dental floss?**

_____

_____

**Tooth cleaners over the years**

_____

_____

**Tooth Care**

_____

**Tools for cleaning teeth**

_____

_____

_____

**Your favorite toothpaste and floss**

_____

_____

_____

# The Zoo

**Read.**

I like to baby-sit for my little cousins. They are four and one, and they are so adorable. One Thursday, my aunt Sharon asked if I would take the kids to the zoo. I said sure and invited a couple of my friends along to help.

We had the best time! My aunt gave us $20 to spend at the zoo. Then she said she would pick us up in four hours. That may sound like a long time, but it wasn't at all. We still weren't ready to go home by the time she came to get us.

We walked through half of the zoo right away. My cousin Will only knows a few words, but he loves animals. He pointed at the animals and shouted words that only he understood. We all laughed at him, and he liked that. Will really liked the little sparrows hopped around on the sidewalk. He yelled at the birds and told us, "Buh-buh." Will's other favorites were the monkeys. He laughed and laughed when we saw them. He even jumped around and acted like them.

After a while, everyone started to get hot and tired. We decided to take a break and have some lunch. The kids each had a hot dog. My friends and I each ate a hot pretzel and we all shared a soda. My cousin Amy cried because she couldn't have ice cream, but we promised her we would do other fun things with the rest of the money.

After lunch, we saw the rest of the zoo. The lions roared as we watched them. My friends and I tried to copy the sounds they made. That made Will and Amy laugh. Will tried it too, but he just sounded like a dog barking.

After we had seen all of the animals, we went to the gift shop. Amy asked for a small lion figure. She collects zoo animals. We bought her one and got Will some stretchy frogs. The frogs were only about as long as my thumb, but you could stretch their legs until they were as long as my arm. We spent a long time in the gift shop just playing with them.

When there was only about half an hour left, we went to the zoo playground and stayed there until my aunt arrived. My friends and I agreed that this had been the best baby-sitting job ever. The kids slept the whole way home in their car seats.

**Answer the questions.**

1. Who is telling the story?

   _____

2. How old do you think the storyteller is? Explain your answer.

   _____

3. How old are Amy and Will?

   _____

4. Who is younger, Amy or Will?

   _____

5. Do you know if the baby-sitter is a boy or a girl?

   _____

6. Has the storyteller baby-sat for Amy and Will before this time? Circle the parts of the story that tell you the answer.

   _____

7. List four things the kids did at the zoo.

   _____

   _____

   _____

8. What time of year is it? Circle the parts of the story that tell you the answer.

   _____

# Limericks

Limericks are fun poems with a specific rhyme pattern and rhythm. They are usually silly and sometimes disgusting. Here are two limericks written by Edward Lear. Lear was a famous author known for his nonsense poems and limericks.

*There was an Old Man with a beard,*
*Who said, "It is just as I feared!—*
*Two Owls and a Hen,*
*Four Larks and a Wren,*
*Have all built their nests in my beard!"*

*There was an old man of Blackheath,*
*Whose head was adorned with a wreath,*
*Of lobsters and spice,*
*Pickled onions and mice,*
*That uncommon old man of Blackheath.*

**The first, second, and last lines end with the same rhyme. The third and fourth lines are shorter and rhyme with each other. The first and last lines are often similar.**

**When you try to write a limerick, follow these steps.**

**Step 1:** Think of an unusual character and a funny-sounding place.
**Step 2:** Think of a word that rhymes with the place.
**Step 3:** Think of a problem—a crazy thing the character did or the crazy way he looks.
**Step 4:** The third and fourth lines briefly tell what happened because of the problem.
**Step 5:** The last line repeats the first line with a variation resulting from the problem.

**Example:**
Character: crazy bird
Place: Peru
Rhyme with Peru: shoe
Problem: bird lived in a shoe
Result: bird was flattened by a foot

*There was a crazy bird from Peru,*
*Who thought the best home was a shoe.*
*He was as snug as a pin,*
*When a foot crowded in.*
*That poor, flat bird from Peru.*

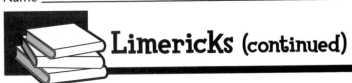

# Limericks (continued)

**Write your own limerick. Start by planning your limerick.**

Interesting character: _____

Fun-sounding place: _____

Rhyme with place: _____

Problem: _____

Result: _____

**Use the information above to write your limerick.**

(Rhyme)

(a)     Line 1

        _____

(a)     Line 2

        _____

(b)     Line 3

        _____

(b)     Line 4

        _____

(a)     Line 5

        _____

# Nonsense Words

using context clues

**There is a nonsense word in each pair of sentences. Write the word on the line that makes sense in place of the nonsense word.**

1. Isabel and Brett rode their bikes to the *flibber* down the street.
   We watched Gretchen *flibber* the car in the driveway.

   The nonsense word *flibber* means _____.

2. The little white dog is Tyrone's new *prackle*.
   Would you like to *prackle* this snake?

   The nonsense word *prackle* means _____.

3. My mom told me to *tirth* the baby to sleep.
   When we were on the beach, I found a beautiful *tirth* with a fossil leaf imprint.

   The nonsense word *tirth* means _____.

4. Don't step on the *blape* on the sidewalk!
   While making breakfast, I can *blape* the eggs into the pan.

   The nonsense word *blape* means _____.

5. I can't chew gum because it will *verg* to my braces.
   My dad asked me to pick up every *verg* in the yard.

   The nonsense word *verg* means _____.

6. I can read the time on my new *jeffa*.
   Will you *jeffa* me at my swim meet?

   The nonsense word *jeffa* means _____.

# Ellie and Polly

**Read.**

Ellie and Polly walked in the hot sun. Ellie was sweating, but she kept walking happily. Polly didn't know where they were going, but she would go where Ellie went. When they arrived at the shop, there was a long line. Ellie and Polly got in line. Ellie looked ahead. There were 10 people ahead of them. It was so hot! It sure was hard to wait!

Polly looked around at the people. She noticed a white dog that looked interesting. She wanted to go see that dog, but Ellie grabbed her collar and said, "No, stay here with me."

Ellie looked ahead. Now there were only five people ahead of them in line. Ellie looked up at the wall. She knew just what she wanted. She wiped the sweat off her forehead. Polly was hot, too.

Ellie was excited. They were next in line. Polly brushed up against Ellie's leg as if to push her ahead. Ellie scratched Polly's neck. "You're right, girl, it is our turn." Ellie walked up to the counter and said, "I'll have a single scoop of chocolate chip, please. And may I have a bowl of water for my friend?"

**Circle yes or no.**

| | | |
|---|---|---|
| 1. Ellie and Polly are both children. | **yes** | **no** |
| 2. Polly is a dog. | **yes** | **no** |
| 3. It is a hot summer day. | **yes** | **no** |
| 4. Ellie and Polly are walking to school. | **yes** | **no** |
| 5. Ellie is sweating because she is nervous. | **yes** | **no** |
| 6. They are at a record store. | **yes** | **no** |
| 7. Ellie is buying ice cream. | **yes** | **no** |
| 8. Ellie is three years old. | **yes** | **no** |
| 9. Polly is excited. | **yes** | **no** |

**Draw a picture of Ellie and Polly.**

# Making Money

**Read.**

Every year, the fifth graders at Brookstone Elementary go on a field trip to Washington, D.C. Rob Kolbe has heard about the trip from his fifth-grade friends. He knows that they see the White House and visit the Smithsonian. Rob is really looking forward to going next year, but his mom and dad won't give him the money for the trip.

Rob asks his mom and dad if they will pay for half of the trip if he earns the other half of the money himself. His parents agree. Rob has almost a year to earn $150.

Christmas is coming soon and Rob's first idea is to earn money baby-sitting. He types a nice letter with his picture on it. The letter says that he will baby-sit while his neighbors go Christmas shopping. He will baby-sit any kids between the ages of three and seven at his house. He names a few afternoons and a Friday evening when his mom or dad will be home. He gives the hours and says that it will cost $1 per hour per child. When the kids come, Rob plays games with them. After five baby-sitting sessions, Rob has earned $45.

When the warm weather arrives, Rob knocks on his neighbors' doors to ask if they need help with yard work. He helps with mowing and raking. He also weeds gardens. After the summer is over, Rob has earned $75 by helping with yard work.

Rob has spent a little of the money he has earned. When fall arrives, Rob counts his money and determines that he still needs $40 for his trip. Rob's mom sees an advertisement for a job for Rob. He gets a job delivering newspapers every Wednesday afternoon. He makes 5¢ for every paper he delivers. Each Wednesday, he earns $10.

It isn't long before Rob has enough money to go on the trip to Washington, D.C. He is just in time. The class trip is on October 15.

Rob's mom and dad give him a check for the $150 they promised him. Rob gets his money from the bank and brings all of the money to school. What a great feeling! Rob has helped pay for his trip. He can't wait to go.

Name _____

**Answer the questions.**

1. Who are the characters mentioned in the story?

   _____

2. Who is the main character?

   _____

3. Write a sentence that describes the main character.

   _____

4. What is the problem in the story?

   _____

5. What solution does the main character propose?

   _____

6. What are the steps he takes to solve the problem?

   _____

7. Does he reach his goal to solve the problem?

   _____

8. How does the main character feel about the solution to the problem?

   _____

9. If you were Rob, what would you have done?

   _____

   _____

   _____

   _____

# Mermaid or Sea Cow?

fact or opinion

**Read.**

Long ago, lonely sailors at sea made up stories of beautiful mermaids who were part human and part fish. These mermaids would sing songs to the lonely sailors. The sailors had to watch out for these mermaids who would lure them to crash on the rocks. The stories were inspired by the large sea animals called manatees.

Manatees are also called "sea cows," which is a pretty good description of what they look like. They are large but gentle animals that float in the sea and graze in the water. Manatees make high-pitched sounds.

Manatees have no enemies except people. Long ago, manatees were hunted for their meat, leathery skin, and their bones. About 100 years ago, the manatee was coming close to extinction.

It is now against the law to hunt manatees, but they are still in danger. People continue to build homes and roads near the manatees' homes and feeding grounds. Manatees can get hurt by speedboat propellers or get tangled up in fishing gear. They are in danger of extinction until people learn more about them.

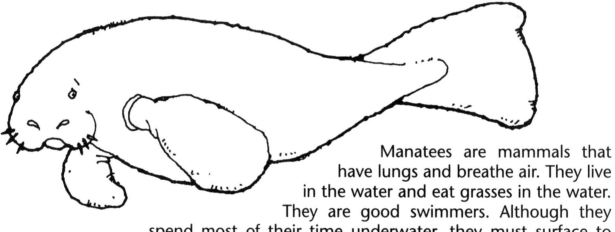

Manatees are mammals that have lungs and breathe air. They live in the water and eat grasses in the water. They are good swimmers. Although they spend most of their time underwater, they must surface to breathe. An active manatee may come up to breathe about every 30 seconds. A resting manatee may only come up every 20 minutes.

Manatees live in shallow waters where they can easily surface to breathe. These shallow areas are also close to people. Many scientists and other caring people are trying to protect the manatees. They put up signs telling people about manatees. They teach children in schools how they can help protect these unique animals. One thing children can do is pick up trash on the shore. Some classrooms even adopt a manatee. They pay a fee and get pictures and information about one manatee. The money is used to teach others about this unusual animal.

*Reading for Understanding*

# Mermaid or Sea Cow? (continued)

fact or opinion

**Sometimes opinions get in the way of helping animals that are in danger.
Cross out the opinions.**

Manatees inspired the sailors' stories of mermaids.

Manatees make high-pitched sounds.

Manatees are big and ugly.

Manatees make a horrible noise.

Manatees are mammals that breathe air.

They live in shallow waters.

Boats are more important than animals.

Manatees eat grasses underwater.

Their only enemy is people.

Hunting is bad.

Hunting manatees is against the law.

It is okay for the manatee to become extinct.

Boat propellers can hurt manatees.

Shallow waters should be used just by people for swimming and boating.

Signs tell people about where manatees live so people can watch out for them.

Children should pick up trash.

Manatees are interesting animals.

# Welcome to the White House

**Cut out and staple the pages in order. Read about the White House.**

## Welcome to the White House

The White House is located at 1600 Pennsylvania Avenue N.W. in Washington, D.C.

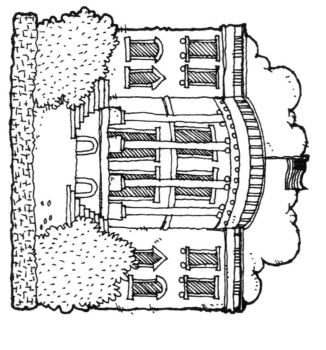

The White House is a historic building with many interesting rooms.
The president of the United States and his family live in the White House.
The president also works there.

1

## The East Room

This nearly empty room is used for parties, dances, weddings, and other ceremonies.

This room has had some unusual uses. Perhaps the strangest was when Theodore Roosevelt used it to host a wrestling match. His children also used it for roller-skating.

2

*Reading for Understanding*

## The State Dining Room

This elegant room seats as many as 140 guests for dinner.

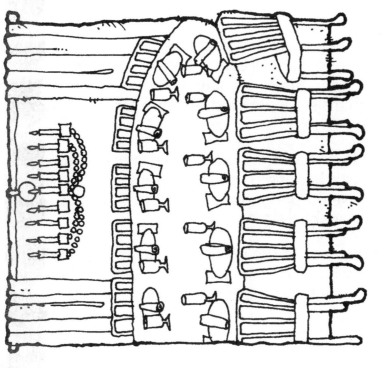

The fireplace mantel is inscribed with a quote from President John Adams:

"I pray Heaven to Bestow the Best of Blessings on THIS HOUSE and on All that shall hereafter Inhabit it. May none but honest and Wise Men ever rule this roof."

4

## The Oval Office

This is the president's formal office.

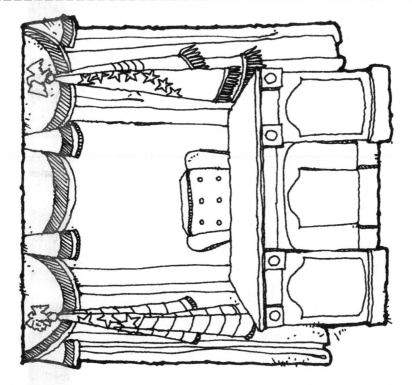

Each president decorates the office to fit his tastes. Some things do not change, though. Two flags (the U.S. flag and the president's flag) always stand behind the president's desk. The presidential seal decorates the ceiling of the Oval Office.

3

 # Plastic

**Read.**

We use plastic every day. Lots of things in our homes such as toys, dishes, shoes, bags, and many containers are made from different kinds of plastics. Scientists have worked hard over the years to make plastic strong and long-lasting. Now they are finding that plastic is not decomposing in our landfills and that garbage dumps are filling up fast. Plastic containers and bags are also polluting our beaches and hurting animals. People must be more careful about how they throw away plastic materials.

One thing we can all do is recycle our plastic containers. Some grocery stores ask customers to return plastic bags used to pack groceries. These bags can be burned because they do not give off poisonous fumes. Other plastics make the air toxic (poisonous) when they are burned.

When you are shopping, look at the bottom of each plastic container you buy. If it has a recycle symbol with a number in it, you know it can be recycled. Find out what numbers of plastic containers your city recycles. If your area does not recycle number-5 plastics, try not to buy products that come in number-5 containers. If you cannot recycle a container, try to use it for something else rather than throwing it away.

When you are done with toys or materials made of plastic, try to think of someone else who could use them. Do you have a neighbor or a cousin who might like what you have outgrown? If you bring items to a secondhand store or have a garage sale, someone else can enjoy your things. Sharing toys and hand-me-downs is a great way to recycle.

Recycling centers sell used plastic to companies that process the plastic and make it into new materials. Some companies make park benches out of recycled plastic. Plastic can also be used to make timbers for walkways, decks, and even some buildings. These plastic products can be made in different colors so you never need to paint them. They also last for a long, long time.

Plastic is not a natural material so it is difficult for it to decompose back into the earth. For that reason, it is important that we find ways to reuse plastic rather than filling up garbage dumps. What creative ways can you think of to reuse plastic?

---

# Plastic (continued)

**Circle fact or opinion after each statement.**

1. Plastic is bad.                                          **fact**     **opinion**

2. Plastic can harm animals.                               **fact**     **opinion**

3. You should recycle plastic.                             **fact**     **opinion**

4. Landfills are ugly.                                     **fact**     **opinion**

5. Plastic decomposes slowly in a landfill.               **fact**     **opinion**

6. Animals are our most precious resource.                **fact**     **opinion**

7. Recycled plastic can be remade into new materials.     **fact**     **opinion**

8. Plastics are the best materials for dishes and containers.  **fact**     **opinion**

9. You should buy your toys at garage sales.              **fact**     **opinion**

10. Hand-me-downs are the best kind of toys.              **fact**     **opinion**

11. Buying number-5 plastic containers is wrong.          **fact**     **opinion**

---

**Draw a picture of a way to reuse something plastic. Be creative.**

# Publishing a Book

**Read.**

My name is Elliot. I am an editor at a publishing house. My job is to find great children's stories and help them get published as books that you can buy or check out at the library. I love my job. Let me tell you all about it.

Many people send me their ideas for books. Some of the ideas are not very good, some are okay, and some are great. I look for the ones that I think are great and that kids like you will love to read. If I like an author's idea, I ask her to send me a copy of her story.

Authors get ideas for stories in many ways. Some write about imaginary things. Others write about things that actually happened. Authors can tell a story just like it really happened, or they can change the events to make it more interesting. As they write, authors try to think of just the right words to tell the story. They might make lists of words, take notes, or make outlines. Sometimes authors need more information to write. Then they go to the library, take field trips, or look up their topics on the Internet. When they write, authors cross out a lot of words that just don't sound right.

When the author is done writing the story, she sends a copy to me. If I like it, I call the author and offer to publish her story. Then I read the story again. I give the author some suggestions for making the story even better. I tell the author what I really like and give suggestions for better words. The author has to read the book to lots of people to get help. The author rewrites the story until it is just right.

When the words are just right, I work with a designer to plan how the book will look. We choose the size of the book, the type, and the style of pictures that will match the story. The designer hires an artist to draw the pictures. The artist does not talk to the author.

When everything is ready, I send the pictures and text to the printer. The printer and binder put all the pieces together and ship the finished books to our warehouse. From the warehouse, we ship the books to stores and libraries all around the world.

I know that you are a writer, too. Does some of what I do look like the work you do when you write? Maybe someday you will send me one of *your* stories.

# Publishing a Book (continued)

sequencing

**Put the steps of the publishing process in order from 1 to 12.**

_____ Editor helps author rewrite the story.

_____ Author gets an idea.

_____ The printer and binder put the book together.

_____ Editor offers to publish the story.

_____ Artist draws pictures.

_____ Editor plans the book with the designer.

_____ Author writes a story.

_____ Designer hires an artist.

_____ Author sends the story to an editor.

_____ The books are shipped all over the world.

_____ Author makes all the words just right.

_____ You buy the book in a bookstore.

**Think about the process you go through when you write. Write the steps you take in your "publishing journey."**

_____

_____

_____

**Which of the steps in your publishing process are just like the steps in the publishing of a children's book?**

_____

_____

_____

# Sharks

**Read.**

When you hear the word "shark" do you think of a fierce hunter—an animal that attacks people ruthlessly? Over the years, the shark has gotten a bad reputation with people. However, there are typically fewer than 12 deaths from shark attacks in any year. Dogs kill more people in one year than sharks have killed in over 200 years. If people understand sharks better, maybe they will not be so afraid of this ocean fish.

Sharks have been around for millions of years. Today there are over 350 different species of sharks. Some sharks are large and live in the open ocean. Other sharks are small and live near the ocean floor. Some sharks are fast swimmers and active hunters, while others are slow creatures that eat tiny fish.

Sharks are fish, but unlike most fish, they do not have bony skeletons. They are mostly muscle with flexible skeletons of soft cartilage. Sharks move constantly in the water in order to breathe. Most fish have gill flaps that force water and oxygen through their gills. Sharks have open gill slits. As they swim, the oxygen-rich water flows through their gills. If a shark gets trapped by a net, it quickly drowns. A shark cannot breathe if it is not moving through the water.

Some sharks, such as the tiger shark, hammerhead shark, and great white shark, are fierce hunters. Their prey may include fish, turtles, seals, dolphins, and small sharks. They can sense sudden movement in the water and smell their prey with their excellent sense of smell. Unless there is a lot of prey in an area, sharks usually hunt alone. When a person is attacked, it is often because the shark thought he was a sea lion, or the shark was warning the human to stay out of its territory. Most people survive shark attacks. The shark usually bites and then swims away.

Many sharks are gentle, harmless fish. The whale shark may grow to be 40 feet (12 meters) long. But this giant eats plankton, which is made up of tiny floating organisms such as fish, shrimp, and larvae. Some sharks are just inches long and eat worms and clams.

Unfortunately, some species of sharks are disappearing. Because sharks are feared, they have been hunted greatly. Sharks are hunted for their meat and skin. Large sharks hold up to 100 gallons of oil in their livers. That oil is used for many purposes. Each year, millions of sharks are caught in nets meant for other fish. Water pollution is also killing sharks as well as other marine life. It is sad to watch the decline of this diverse order of fish that has been around for millions of years.

# Sharks (continued)

**Circle true or false after each statement.**

| | | | |
|---|---|---|---|
| 1. | Sharks attack and kill hundreds of people each year. | **true** | **false** |
| 2. | Sharks have been around for millions of years. | **true** | **false** |
| 3. | Sharks are all fierce hunters. | **true** | **false** |
| 4. | There are thousands of different species of sharks. | **true** | **false** |
| 5. | Not all sharks are fast swimmers. | **true** | **false** |
| 6. | Sharks breathe through gill slits. | **true** | **false** |
| 7. | Sharks drown if they stop swimming. | **true** | **false** |
| 8. | Sharks do not have bony skeletons. | **true** | **false** |
| 9. | Sharks are made of mostly fat and oil. | **true** | **false** |
| 10. | Sharks usually hunt in groups, called schools. | **true** | **false** |
| 11. | The whale shark eats plankton. | **true** | **false** |
| 12. | Sharks are not in danger of disappearing. | **true** | **false** |
| 13. | Sharks are hunted for their meat. | **true** | **false** |
| 14. | Pollution is not dangerous to sharks. | **true** | **false** |

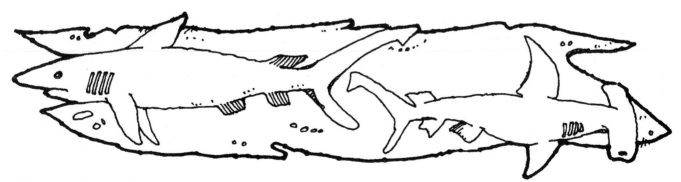

**Did you know?**

A shark's skin is rough like sandpaper. It is covered with scales that are a lot like your teeth. The scales are different shapes on different parts of the body. On fast-swimming sharks, the scales are spaced far apart so they don't slow it down in the water.

Name _____

**Read.**

In the 19th century, many pioneers moved to the American West to start new lives. When they finally found the land where they wanted to settle, there were many important tasks to be done. They had to plant gardens and crops. They had to dig wells. Maybe they needed to prepare for winter. Since there were so many things to do, they often built temporary houses. Their homes had to be strong enough to protect them but not take too long to build. In a few years, when their lives were more established and they had money to buy materials, the pioneers would build more permanent homes.

One kind of temporary home was a sod house. Sod houses were built where trees were scarce and were made of packed dirt. The dirt was cut right from the ground with plows and axes into brick shapes. As they plowed their fields, the pioneers skimmed off the top layer of tough sod to use for the sod bricks. At the same time, they freed up the looser soil below for planting. The sod bricks were thick with roots. The pioneers stacked them together much like regular bricks to form the house. As the sod house settled, it became stronger. The roots helped cement the bricks together as they grew from one brick into another.

The well-made soddy was comfortable and dry. Windows and doors were made with wooden frames, and real glass was often used. A roof could be made with straw and dirt, or a wooden roof could be covered with more sod. The sod house stayed cool in the summer and warm in the winter. A poorly made soddy leaked when it rained and allowed wind through the cracks.

Sod house residents often had company in their homes. Snakes, insects, and other small critters were very comfortable in the sod bricks. It was not uncommon to see a snake making itself at home on the window sill or to see a mouse scurrying around on the floor. Other creatures and bits of dirt often dropped from the ceiling.

The pioneers were strong people who worked hard and fought to survive in rugged places. They were clever in their use of natural resources. Their use of the sod house is just one symbol of their determination to make it in the Wild West.

# Sod Houses (continued)

**Follow the outline to take notes on the article "Sod Houses."**

## First Paragraph

Main idea _____

Details _____

_____

## Second Paragraph

Main idea _____

Details _____

_____

## Third Paragraph

Main idea _____

Details _____

_____

## Fourth Paragraph

Main idea _____

Details _____

_____

## Fifth Paragraph

Main idea _____

Details _____

_____

Name _____

# The *Mayflower*

**Read.**

Imagine leaving behind your home and all your things to sail across the ocean to a new world where there are no towns and no homes. Do you think you would be scared? Excited? This is what the passengers of the *Mayflower* faced in their journey from England to America in the year 1620.

The *Mayflower* traveled for 66 days across the unpredictable Atlantic Ocean. The ship carried 102 passengers and nearly 30 crew members. The passengers were the people who were riding on the boat from England to America. The sailors, or crew, were the people who worked on the ship. The crew planned to return to England once the passengers were settled.

The *Mayflower* was a fairly small ship for so many people. The passengers slept, ate, and lived in the area called "the 'tween decks" (between decks). The 'tween decks was one large space, beneath the main deck, about the size of a volleyball court. It was crowded, wet, and dark there. The passengers did not leave this area often. They even cooked there in small boxes using charcoal. This was difficult in rough weather. They ate oatmeal, hard biscuits, dried fruit, rice, and salted beef brought with them from England. Many of the passengers became seasick during the trip. Occasionally, when the weather was calm, they would go up on deck to stretch their legs. The sailors preferred them to stay below and out of their way.

Every sailor was busy with the job of maintaining the ship. Some sailors climbed high on the mast to the lookout. Others put the sails up or down and repaired torn sails. The captain and his officers read maps in the round room. They used navigational tools on the half deck to determine where they were. Some sailors steered the boat. Others cooked for the crew in the forecastle. Many of the sailors helped to keep the boat clean. The sailors were paid well, but it was hard work. They had to leave their families for months at a time. The trip was dangerous and the food wasn't very good. The sailors often worked for four hours then slept for four hours in shifts around the clock.

When the ship landed in the Plymouth harbor, the passengers started the difficult task of settling in. They needed to build homes and get ready for the coming winter. They had to depend on each other to get the work done. Even the children had to work hard.

As soon as the passengers were settled, the crew of the *Mayflower* began the long, hard journey back to England.

Name _____

 # The *Mayflower* (continued)

**Answer the questions in complete sentences.**

1. Why do you think the sailors were paid so well? List three reasons.

   _____

   _____

   _____

2. Why would sailors choose the job of sailing across the ocean?

   _____

3. Why would passengers choose to sail all the way to America?

   _____

4. What made the journey difficult for the passengers?

   _____

5. Why didn't the passengers go up on deck very often?

   _____

6. What kept the sailors busy during the trip?

   _____

7. How was the trip on the *Mayflower* different from a trip on a big ship today?

   Food: _____

   Sleeping: _____

   Fresh air: _____

   How the ship was powered: _____

8. What do you think will be hard for the passengers in their new land?

   _____

   _____

# The *Titanic*

**Read.**

The *Titanic* was one of the finest ships ever built. It was built to be comfortable and luxurious. It was like a floating palace. What was life like on this expensive ship that only sailed on one voyage?

There were three levels of tickets. The most expensive tickets were for "first class." The next level was for "second class." The least expensive tickets were for those traveling in "third class" or "steerage."

The 329 "first-class" passengers had four decks on which to move around. They had cabins with sitting rooms. They could also visit with friends in several different lounges, restaurants, and dining rooms. They had a gym, a pool, a Turkish bath, a library, and beautiful sunny decks. Their meals were made from the fanciest and most expensive foods, such as mutton chops, galantine of chicken, and apple meringue. Dinners consisted of many courses. First-class passengers could choose their meals from a menu. They ate at tables decorated with china plates, crystal, and fresh flowers. Some people wrote about what the ship was like. It was even fancier than what most rich people had at home.

The 285 "second-class" passengers were treated like the first-class passengers on other ships. They had nice cabins, but they were small. They ate a four-course meal each evening on nice tables with pretty plates. They could also go on deck to walk around or sit in the sun. They did not have the restaurants, gyms, and other special rooms of the first class. Their decks were smaller because they held the lifeboats.

The 710 "third-class" passengers had space in the noisy rear of the ship below second class. There were only 220 cabins in "steerage." These cabins were used for families. The other passengers slept in large rooms. The men were in one room and the women were in a second room. The steerage sitting room was a large, plain room with benches and tables. Third-class passengers had to take turns eating in a dining room that sat only 473 people at a time. A ticket told them when to eat. If they missed their time, these passengers went hungry until the next meal. There were no restaurants for them.

Most of the passengers knew that they were on a special trip. The *Titanic* was supposed to be the finest boat ever made. Some very rich and famous people were on the ship for its first trip. Of course, no one on board knew that the boat was going to sink. This probably made the *Titanic*'s first and only trip across the ocean the most famous voyage ever.

Name _____

# The *Titanic* (continued)

**Answer the questions in complete sentences.**

**1.** How do meals in first class differ from meals in second class?

_____

_____

**2.** What was in the first-class cabins that was not in the second- or third-class cabins?

_____

**3.** How did the sleeping rooms in third class compare to those in first and second class?

_____

_____

_____

**4.** What did all passengers know about this trip?

_____

**Read the words of each passenger. Write whether the passenger is first-class (1), second-class (2), or third-class (3).**

_____ "I love my room. I have a beautiful bedroom with a private sitting room."

_____ "My favorite meal is dinner when we have a delicious four-course meal."

_____ "We swam for hours in the pool."

_____ "In the evening, we sit on benches in the only room we all share. We play music and dance."

_____ "I love to sit on the deck in the sun. My brother likes to play under the lifeboats."

_____ "We had a nice meal. We had to eat a little fast so the next group of people could come in and eat."

# Tipi

**Read.**

For thousands of years, people have lived on the Great Plains of the United States and Canada. The Great Plains is a huge expanse of flat, grassy land with few trees. Many different animals used to roam on the plains. The groups of people who lived there would travel around and follow the animals to hunt. They needed homes that they could tear down and set up pretty quickly. Many Plains tribes, such as the Arapaho, Pawnee, Blackfoot, Sioux, and Cheyenne, built tipis to use as homes.

For many years, the tipi was made of wood poles and buffalo hides. When the buffalo became scarce, Plains people used canvas cloth to cover the tipi frame.

The first step in making a tipi was to find and prepare the poles. It took 15 poles to make just one tipi. The poles for the frame had to be long and straight. The best trees for this purpose were willow, lodgepole pine, and cedar. The branches and bark were cut off so they did not poke holes in the tipi cover. When the people traveled with their homes, the poles dragged on the ground. The poles wore out and had to be replaced every year or two.

To prepare the buffalo hides, the women worked together on many steps. First, they scraped and cleaned the inside and outside of each hide. Then they soaked the hides with water to soften them. Next, they sewed as many as 14 hides together in the shape of a half circle. They cut a hole for the door and created smoke flaps. Finally, they fitted the cover over the frame and lit a fire inside. The smoke from the fire helped to preserve the skin. Some tipis were decorated with designs and symbols.

When the Plains people settled in an area, they set up their tipis in a circle. Each family had its place in the circle. The women set up their tipis so the doors faced the morning sun in the east. The backs of the tipis faced the west wind.

In the late 1800s, life on the Plains changed a lot. Many roads and cities began to fill the area. The buffalo were almost all gone. Many of the Plains people were forced to live on reservations. They no longer lived in tipis. Still, the tipi remains an important part of Native American culture today.

# Tipi (continued)

## Answer the questions in complete sentences.

1. What caused the Plains people to move around so much?

   _____

2. How did their lifestyle of moving affect their style of home?

   _____

3. What caused them to use canvas instead of buffalo hides for tipi covers?

   _____

4. What would be the effect of leaving the bark and branches on the tipi poles?

   _____

5. What was the effect on the poles when they were dragged on the ground?

   _____

6. What was the effect of water on the buffalo hides?

   _____

7. What was the effect of smoke on the buffalo hides?

   _____

8. Why did the women face their tipi doors to the east?

   _____

9. What caused the change in life for the Plains people in the late 1800s?

   _____

10. Why do you think it is important to preserve the culture of the Plains people? What would be the effect of the loss?

   _____

   _____

Create a model of a tipi using materials available to you. You will need a half circle of heavy fabric or paper to create the tipi cover. For the frame, you will need up to 14 sticks or poles. Decorate the tipi cover with Native American designs.

# Wolves

**Read.**

If you have been reading fairy tales, you may believe that all wolves are vicious, evil, and ruthless. They eat children and pigs and other small animals. They are aggressive and won't stop until they get what they want. There really isn't anything good to say about wolves. Or is there? Are wolves just misunderstood?

Wolves are actually nothing like the characters portrayed in fairy tales. While it is true that their diet consists of deer, rabbits, and other small animals, wolves would never attack a child just for the sake of eating. Wolves have been known to attack people when the people threaten them. This happens only rarely. Wolves are usually pretty shy animals. They stay within their own territory and protect their own pack.

Wolves are meat-eaters, and they must hunt to get their food. They are strong and fast and have sharp teeth. They use their sense of smell to find prey. Wolves hunt in packs and chase their prey until it gets tired. They usually hunt the weakest, slowest animal in a group. Wolves are not cruel; they are just good hunters.

Some wolves, such as the red wolf, are near extinction. Their homes are steadily disappearing as people spread their own homes further into the wilderness. Wolves have also been hunted extensively.

Ranchers and farmers pose another threat to wolves. They become angry when wolves come onto their property and eat their chickens and sheep. This is a serious problem, because the farmers lose their animals, and the wolves get shot by the angry farmers. No one wins in this battle.

Wolves are an important part of the balance of nature. They hunt weak animals and help keep down the populations of some animals such as deer. In many countries, it is now against the law to hunt wolves. Many zoos and scientists are working hard to protect wolves, because they understand just how important and misunderstood they really are.

# Wolves (continued)

organizing information

Organize the information about wolves into a chart. Compare what makes people think wolves are cruel with what is positive about wolves.

| Negative Characteristics | Positive Characteristics |
|---|---|
| | |

Choose one of the negative characteristics from your chart. Write an explanation of why the wolf needs that trait. Explain why it is not cruel but natural.

_____

_____

_____

Write a brief version of a fairy tale from the wolf's point of view.

_____

_____

_____

_____

_____

_____

# Yellowstone Fires

**Read.**

In 1988, Yellowstone National Park had a huge fire that burned nearly half of the park. Although this may sound like a terrible tragedy, the fires were actually a healthy part of the forest's natural life cycle.

The fires in Yellowstone had to happen. For hundreds of years the forests had been growing without any large fires. Over the years, many trees had grown and died. The tree trunks fell on the ground and stayed there. Eventually the ground was covered with dead trees. This blocked the sun from new growth on the forest floor. It also made it difficult for animals to move around in the forest. The park was becoming covered with forests. There were fewer meadows for new plants, and animals had less area for grazing.

Lightning started several fires in Yellowstone National Park during the dry summer of 1988. The dead tree trunks on the forest floor ignited just like firewood. The fires grew and grew. Firefighters worked hard to control the fires, but they could not stop them. They were able to protect some areas from burning, but the fires did not stop until some snow fell in September. Nature started the fires and nature put them out in the end.

After the fires were out, the forests began to grow again. In some ways, the forests were better off after the fire. Some roots and seeds had remained safe underground during the fires. Others, like lodgepole pine seeds, had been locked in cones that the heat from the fire released. The new plants that grew were not only beautiful, they were also perfect food for the animals that had survived the fire. Most of the animals did survive the fire. Many of them prefer to live in the meadows that now cover much of the park. More than half of the 2.2-million-acre park was untouched by the fires, so there are still plenty of forests for the animals, too.

Yellowstone National Park continues to grow and recover from the huge fires of 1988. As the park grows, new animals and plants find their homes there. In about 300 years, the park will be ready for a new fire to give it a fresh start once again.

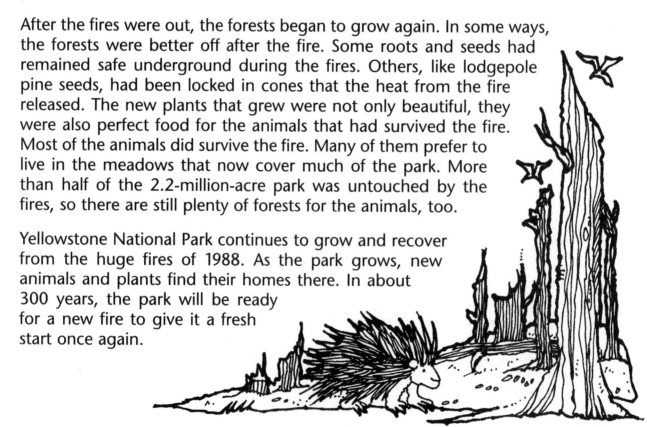

# Yellowstone Fires (continued)

**Write your answers on the lines provided.**

1. What is the effect of a fire on trees and plants in a forest?

   _____

2. What caused the fires to start in Yellowstone?

   _____

3. What is the effect on the forest if there are no fires for years?

   _____

4. What caused the fires to spread so quickly?

   _____

5. What caused the lodgepole pinecones to open up and release their seeds?

   _____

6. Why did the animals return to the site of the fires?

   _____

7. What will be the effect of 300 more years of growth?

   _____

8. Was the effect of the Yellowstone fires positive or negative? Explain your answer.

   _____

   _____

9. Why was it so difficult for animals to move around in the forest before the fires?

   _____

10. What caused the Yellowstone fires to stop?

   _____

# Listening to Music

**As you read the story, you will be asked some questions. Answer the questions you can before reading ahead. Go back to answer the others after reading more.**

Shobu loved to listen to music. He had a collection of 150 CDs. As soon as he came home from school, he turned on his music. Shobu was an excellent student, so his mother let him listen to music while he did his homework.

Shobu's father was a judge. He worked long hours at the courthouse and came home very tired. In the evening, Shobu's music bothered Mr. Agrawal. One day, Mr. Agrawal told Shobu that he could no longer listen to his music after six o'clock in the evening. This was bad news for Shobu, but he turned off his music.

1.  *How do you think Shobu feels about turning off his music?*

    _____

2.  *What steps do you think Shobu will take next?*

    _____

3.  *After reading: What did Shobu do?*

    _____

    _____

Shobu wanted his father to be happy, but he also missed his rock music. He asked his father if it would be all right if he listened to his music on a personal CD player with headphones. Shobu's father agreed.

As soon as dinner was over, Shobu put on his headphones. He washed the dishes with his headphones on. He did his homework listening to his CDs that no one else could hear. This worked out well for everyone.

One day, Shobu's father asked him a question about his homework. Shobu did not hear his father because he was wearing his headphones. Mr. Agrawal grew angry. The headphones made Shobu seem like he wasn't interested in the rest of the family. Mr. Agrawal told him that he could not listen to music while he did his homework. This was bad news for Shobu, but he turned off his music.

4.  *How do you think Shobu feels about turning off his music?*

    _____

# Listening to Music (continued)

**5.** *What steps do you think Shobu will take next?*

_____

**6.** *After reading: What did Shobu do?*

_____

_____

Shobu continued to listen to music on his personal CD player while he did the dishes and other chores. One day, as Shobu reached up high to put away some clean dishes, his headphone cord got caught on the silverware drawer. The cord jerked across Shobu's arm, and he dropped the dishes that he was holding. They broke all over the floor.

Mr. and Mrs. Agrawal came running into the kitchen. When they learned what had happened, they decided to take the CD player away from Shobu. Shobu finished the dishes in silence.

Shobu loved music so much that he felt he must listen to something. He proposed to his parents that he be allowed to listen to his own music in his room until dinnertime. After dinner, they would turn on either classical music or Indian music that everyone could enjoy. Mr. and Mrs. Agrawal knew that music was important to Shobu so they agreed.

**7.** *How did Shobu handle the problem?*

_____

**8.** *Do you think Shobu's parents did the right thing?*

_____

**9.** *What do you think happened the next day?*

_____

**10.** *What is your favorite music?* _____

**11.** *When do you listen to music?*_____

**12.** *Are there any rules about music in your house?*

_____

_____

# Ty Cobb

**Read.**

Many people argue about whether Ty Cobb was the greatest baseball player of all time. But everyone agrees that he was the meanest player of all time.

Ty Cobb played most of his 24-year professional career for the Detroit Tigers at the beginning of the 1900s. He was the game's fiercest competitor both on and off the field. His temper and attitude provoked injuries and fights with other players and sometimes even with his own teammates. Legend has it that Cobb sharpened his spikes before every game to intimidate and even injure other players. He firmly believed that he "owned" the base paths and often proclaimed that no opposing player was going to get in his way.

Cobb had good reason to believe that he did own the base paths. His stolen-base record of 96 in 1915 stood for 47 years. His batting accomplishments are also legendary. He had a lifetime average of .366. He hit 295 triples. He boasted 4,189 hits. He held 12 batting titles (including nine in a row). Cobb played 23 straight seasons in which he hit over .300. During three of those seasons he hit over .400, topped by a .420 mark in 1911. His stats include 1,938 RBI, 2,246 runs, and the Triple Crown in 1909. Cobb led the league five times in stolen bases; his batting average was tops for nine consecutive years (1907–1915) and 12 times in all. He stole 892 bases in his 24 years at bat.

Ty Cobb, also known as "The Georgia Peach," was the first player elected into the Baseball Hall of Fame. He even beat out the legendary and popular Babe Ruth. When he retired, he "owned" virtually every hitting record that was kept. Although people love to hate Ty Cobb, he was a baseball player to remember.

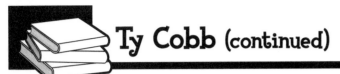

# Ty Cobb (continued)

**Answer the questions in complete sentences.**

1. What did Ty Cobb do that was mean?

   _____

2. Why was Cobb elected to the Baseball Hall of Fame?

   _____

3. What does it mean that Cobb "owned" base paths and records?

   _____

4. What was Ty Cobb's nickname?

   _____

**It can be difficult to read statistics in a paragraph. Plot some of Ty Cobb's statistics on the chart below. Add as many columns as you like. Label the chart and fill in the relevant details.**

# Scientific Classification

**Read.**

Imagine going to the library to check out a book about zebras. When you get to the library, you find that none of the books on the shelves are in any special order. If the library has thousands of books, it could take you weeks to find your book! That is why the library has a very careful classification system. The world of living things on earth also has a careful classification system.

As scientists study living things, they put them into groups with other living things that have similar characteristics. This helps scientists study living things better. A scientist named Carolus Linnaeus (born Carl von Linné in 1707) invented the system of classification that we use today. In this system, every living thing has a common name and a Latin name. The Latin name is made up of a group name and an individual name. New living things are studied and classified into this system every year.

All living things are classified into five large groups called kingdoms. The moneran kingdom contains single-celled organisms without a nucleus, like bacteria and blue-green algae. The protist kingdom is made up of single-celled organisms with a nucleus. The fungi kingdom contains organisms like molds, mildew, and mushrooms. These organisms are different from plants because they do not make their own food. The plant kingdom is made up of organisms that use water and sunlight to make their own food through a process called photosynthesis. The animal kingdom is made up of organisms that move around to find food and to escape danger.

Each of the five kingdoms is further divided into groups called phyla. Phyla are divided into smaller groups called classes. Classes are divided into orders. Orders are divided into families. Families are divided into genera. Within each genus are individual species that are unique from all other groups of living things. For example, the tiger species belongs to the genus of panthers, the family of cats, the order of carnivores, the class of mammals, the phylum of vertebrates, and the kingdom of animals.

This system of classification is very useful to scientists and to you for identifying living things. It is helpful to know how living things are alike and different. When you hear that a cat-sized hyrax is related to an elephant, you can find out what the animals have in common by looking at their places in the classification system.

---

# Scientific Classification (continued)

categorizing

Read the following charts and compare how birds are related to reptiles.

| Reptiles | |
|---|---|
| Kingdom | Animals |
| Phylum | Chordates |
| Subphylum | Vertebrates |
| Class | Reptiles (Reptilia) |
| Number of Orders | 4 major |
| Number of Species | About 7,000 |

| Birds | |
|---|---|
| Kingdom | Animals |
| Phylum | Chordates |
| Subphylum | Vertebrates |
| Class | Birds (Aves) |
| Number of Orders | 23 |
| Number of Species | About 9,000 |

1. How are birds and reptiles the same? How are they different?

   _____

   _____

   _____

2. To what kingdom does each of the following species belong? Write the correct letter in the space next to each species name.

## Kingdoms

| Moneran (M) | Protist (Pr) | Fungi (F) | Plant (Pl) | Animal (A) |
|---|---|---|---|---|

_____ yellow rose       _____ oak tree       _____ single-celled blue-green algae

_____ starfish          _____ human          _____ portabella mushroom

_____ ostrich           _____ centipede      _____ single-celled amoeba
                                                    (with nucleus)

3. Name five species of insects.

   _____   _____   _____   _____   _____

4. Name five species of birds.

   _____   _____   _____   _____   _____

 # Sailing in a Storm

**Read.**

Tina and her dad loved to go sailing together. One summer, they decided to sail to Beaver Island. They put the boat in the water in Charlevoix, Michigan, around six o'clock on a Thursday night. They planned to dock the boat, shop and eat in town, then set out for the island in the morning. Unfortunately, the marina didn't have any available docks for their boat. They had no other choice but to motor across the lake to the island that night.

Mr. Peterson and Tina motored the 23-foot sailboat through the channel and out into Lake Michigan. It was a quiet evening. The sky was clear and there was no wind. Mr. Peterson put up the sails, but they just flopped lightly in the calm air. The motor pushed them across the wide water. They listened to music and ate cheese and avocado sandwiches.

Around ten o'clock, a brisk wind picked up suddenly. They turned off the motor and sailed with the wind. Very quickly, the wind grew too strong and the waves became large. The small boat leaned over and moved quickly through the water as the wind filled the sails.

When water started splashing into the boat, Mr. Peterson shouted, "We have to take down the sails! I can't handle this much wind!" Tina was scared. Her dad wanted her to go up on deck and take down the sails. She was afraid that a wave might wash her overboard or that she might lose her balance. She decided to stay back and steer the boat instead. But Tina didn't like that either. It was hard to control the boat in the strong wind.

Mr. Peterson went up on deck to take down the sails. Tina was shivering. The cold water was soaking her each time the boat crashed through a wave. She was shaking more from fear than cold. What would she do if her dad fell into the water? She didn't think she could turn the boat around to get him. She wondered if they would ever make it to the island.

Once Mr. Peterson had tied up the sails, he took over the steering. Soon the waves grew smaller, the wind died down, and several stars appeared in the sky as the clouds moved away. They motored ahead in silence.

When the island came into sight, Tina sat on the bow of the boat and watched. She thought nothing had ever looked so beautiful as the island with its sheltered bay. They anchored the boat in the bay and put up a mooring light. They unrolled their sleeping bags inside the cabin and fell quickly to sleep.

# Sailing in a Storm (continued)

**Answer the questions in complete sentences.**

1. Do you think Tina and her dad had been sailing before this trip? Explain your answer.

   _____

   _____

2. How do you think Tina and her dad felt when they had to sail to the island that night? Explain your answer.

   _____

   _____

3. When they first started out, there was no wind. How do you think they felt?

   _____

4. When the wind began to pick up, what did Tina and her dad do?

   _____

5. When the wind got too strong, they had a choice to make. What was that choice and what did they choose to do?

   _____

6. After the storm calmed down, Tina and Mr. Peterson did not talk. Why do you think they were so quiet?

   _____

7. Why did the island look so beautiful to Tina?_____

8. What do you think they will do in the morning? _____

9. What sounds do you think you would hear in the storm on the lake?

   _____

   _____

10. What made Tina shiver?_____

 # John Adams

**Read.**

The first president to live in the White House in Washington, D.C. was John Adams. John Adams was the first vice president of the United States and the second president. When the United States was becoming a country in the late 1700s, John Adams was an important person.

When the country was new, elections for president were different. In today's elections, a presidential candidate chooses a running mate that will become vice president if the team receives the most votes. In the late 1700s, the presidential candidate with the second largest number of votes became vice president. George Washington was the first president and John Adams was his vice president. When John Adams ran for president in 1796, he had the most votes and Thomas Jefferson had the second most. They made an interesting pair because Jefferson and Adams were rivals. They were also friends who respected each other even though they disagreed about many issues.

The 1796 election was the first election to have two political parties: the Federalists and the Democratic-Republicans. John Adams was a Federalist. It was very important to him that the country not fight in a war with the French. The Federalist Party did not last very long past John Adams. The Democrats and the Republicans are the two major parties in the United States now.

Before running for president, John Adams was the head of the committee that wrote the Declaration of Independence. The Declaration of Independence is a written statement that says the United States is its own country, not a colony of Britain. With this statement, the people of the United States no longer would be under the rule of the British King or Britain's laws. They established their own laws and procedures. We still celebrate the day the Declaration of Independence was signed on the Fourth of July. John Adams was the leader of the group in Congress that wanted to make the United States an independent country.

John Adams was president for four years. Several years later, his son John Quincy Adams also became president. They were the first father and son to both serve as president. More than 200 years later, the next father and son presidents were George Bush and George W. Bush.

John Adams was a great man in U.S. history. He worked hard for the country and spent many years away from his family for his job. That was very difficult for him, but serving his country was extremely important to him.

# John Adams (continued)

## Complete the activities.

1. Draw an **X** next to each statement that could be true about John Adams.

   _____ He was excited about being president, because he thought he could make lots of money.

   _____ He rarely offered to help with committees in Congress.

   _____ He was so dedicated to the independence movement that he was rarely home.

   _____ We don't remember much about him, because he didn't do much for this country.

2. Write four words or phrases that describe John Adams.

_____            _____

### JOHN ADAMS

_____            _____

3. Name two big accomplishments of John Adams.

_____

_____

# The Digestive System

**Read.**

Your body needs energy and vitamins and minerals so that it can move and grow. Your body uses food to make your bones strong, your hair shiny, and your muscles strong. How does your body use the food you eat? Your body breaks down the food and sends it to different parts of your body through the process of digestion.

The digestive system starts in your mouth. You chew your food to break it down into small pieces. When you chew, saliva enters your mouth from glands in your cheeks and under your tongue. Saliva also helps the food to break into pieces and turn into a liquid.

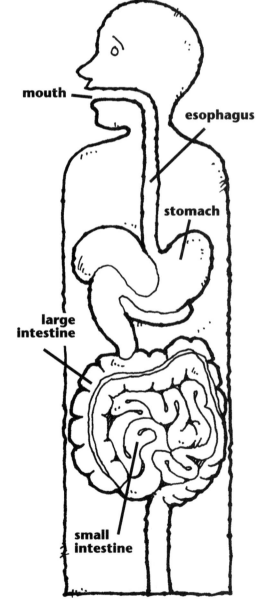

When you swallow, your food goes down your esophagus. This tube starts at the back of your throat and leads to your stomach. Since you also breathe through your mouth, there is another tube, called the trachea (windpipe) that leads to your lungs. That pipe has a little "door" on it that closes when food is coming down.

The esophagus squeezes the food and pushes it down toward the stomach. The stomach is a tube at the bottom of the esophagus. The stomach stretches as it fills with food. Food breaks down even further while in the stomach. The walls of the stomach produce an acidic liquid called gastric juice. The stomach muscles squeeze the food and mix it with the gastric juice until it is mushy. This can take two or more hours.

The mushy food moves into your small intestines next. From there, the food molecules are spread all over your body. The small intestine is surrounded by blood vessels. The food particles flow into the blood vessels and travel to the parts of the body that need them.

Even after all that, there is still some food that has not been digested. Your body cannot use all of the food you eat. Any undigested food is sent to the large intestine. It waits there until you get rid of it in the toilet.

Name _____

# The Digestive System (continued)

**Choose an activity to write in response to the article.**

- Write a story from the point of view of a food particle traveling through the digestive system.

- Write 10 questions that can be answered from reading the selection. Write the answers to the questions on a separate page.

- Draw and label the digestive system.

- Make a chart of the parts of the digestive system. In one column, write the part. In another column, write its function.

- Make a glossary of 10 terms related to the digestive system.

- Write 10 statements that are either true or false about the digestive system. Write the correct answers on a separate page.

- Research the food groups to determine what nutrients different foods provide. Write about the effect these nutrients have on your body.

- Write and perform a song about the process of digestion and the foods that keep us healthy.

- Write a play in which your classmates act out the process of digestion. Be specific about the actions of the actors and the words they say to communicate what they are doing.

Name _____

# Questions and Answers

**Read the questions on the left and the answers on the right.**
**Draw a line from each question to its correct answer.**

"What would you like to have for dinner tonight?"

"My favorite is Spaghetti. I love their music."

"Have you counted the number of trees on the property?"

"Yes, Potter came in first place."

"Have you read any of the Harry Potter books?"

"Lasagna would be my first choice."

"What is your favorite rock band?"

"I read that there are 898. It is surrounded by 50 U.S. flags."

"How many steps are there on the way to the top of the Washington Monument?"

"Yes, I read the first and second. They were both exciting."

"Did you see Potter running in the race around the lake?"

"Yes, there are 14 maples, 10 oaks, and 2 others I don't recognize."

*Reading for Understanding*

Name _____

# Comprehension Review Test

**Fill in the circle next to the best answer.**

> Tara carried lumpy packages under her arms and in both hands. She walked next to her mother who also carried numerous packages. They struggled together to get the door open and fit into the room. They walked just ahead of a fat man in a red suit. As Tara and her mother walked in, they heard a room full of children shout and cheer.

**1.** What time of year does this paragraph take place?

   ○ spring        ○ fall        ○ winter        ○ summer

**2.** Who is the character in the red suit?

   ○ Uncle Sam        ○ Santa        ○ a red fox        ○ Clifford

**3.** What is in the packages?

   ○ homework        ○ presents        ○ groceries        ○ library books

**4.** What are Tara and her mother doing?

   ○ shopping        ○ returning books    ○ bringing gifts        ○ trick-or-treating

> Maddie was falling asleep in the car on her way home from ballet rehearsal. This was the fourth practice this week. She was so happy to be in the Nutcracker this year, but it was hard work. She had a test in math tomorrow and she still needed to do her homework. What should she do?

**5.** What is the problem?

   ○ Maddie is late for school.        ○ Maddie misses her friends.

   ○ Maddie doesn't like ballet.        ○ Maddie is too busy.

**6.** What is the setting?

   ○ a stage        ○ the car        ○ school        ○ a bedroom

**7.** Which is not a good solution?

   ○ bring homework to ballet        ○ talk to her teachers

   ○ don't do her homework        ○ sleep a lot this weekend

# Comprehension Review Test (continued)

Someday we will have people living in space. We hope to have a space station in place so people can live on Mars without space suits. They will grow their own food. They will have schools, places to work, and stores. There will be a whole space community within the space station.

**8.** Which of these is not part of the plan?

- ○ going to school
- ○ flying to other planets
- ○ shopping
- ○ living without space suits

**9.** Which of these is not a fantasy?

- ○ touching the stars
- ○ rocket suits
- ○ space station
- ○ little green martians

Dolphins and porpoises are very much alike. They are both mammals. They breathe air and have lungs, not gills. They both eat fish. Dolphins grow longer and heavier than porpoises do. The snout of a dolphin looks like a bird's beak, while the porpoise has a round and blunt snout. The dolphin has sharp teeth, and the porpoise has teeth shaped like spades. Dolphins can swim twice as fast as porpoises.

**10.** Which sentence tells what is the same about dolphins and porpoises?

- ○ They are both fish.
- ○ They both have lungs.
- ○ They are the same length.
- ○ They both have sharp teeth.

**11.** Which sentence tells what is different about dolphins and porpoises?

- ○ The dolphin is actually a fish.
- ○ The porpoise eats leaves.
- ○ The porpoise is longer than the dolphin.
- ○ The dolphin's snout is more pointed.

Emily has a beautiful dollhouse that her mom and dad gave her when she was four years old. She doesn't play with it anymore. She is thinking about giving it to her little cousin who is turning four next month. Emily wants her cousin to have it, but she also wants to keep it because it is a special toy from her parents. She doesn't know what she should do.

# Comprehension Review Test (continued)

**12.** What is the main idea of the story?

- ○ Emily loves her cousin.
- ○ Emily's dollhouse is beautiful.
- ○ Emily doesn't want the dollhouse.
- ○ Emily doesn't know what to do with her dollhouse.

> Freda looked at the sun as it was going down over the water. She could tell that the days were getting shorter. She knew that she should start getting ready for winter. She was starting to get sleepy and she noticed that her coat was getting thicker. It was almost time for a long winter nap.

**13.** What is Freda?

- ○ a person
- ○ a bear
- ○ a cat
- ○ a bird

**14.** What is Freda doing?

- ○ watching the sunset
- ○ reading a book
- ○ watching TV
- ○ talking to her pet

**15.** Where is Freda?

- ○ in the den
- ○ outside
- ○ in bed
- ○ at a coat store

> There was an old man in a tree,
> Whose whiskers were lovely to see;
> But the birds of the air,
> Pluck'd them perfectly bare,
> To make themselves nests on that tree.
>
> *by Edward Lear*

**16.** Where is the old man?

- ○ in the air
- ○ in a tree
- ○ in a nest
- ○ under a tree

**17.** What did the birds do?

- ○ sat in his hair
- ○ slept in his whiskers
- ○ flew into his tree
- ○ plucked his whiskers

# Reading Rubric

Use this guide to assess students' reading fluency and comprehension. Add descriptors to the rubric that match what you are teaching.

When you assess a student's reading, put a date by each descriptor in the column that best describes the student's performance.

Student: _____

| DESCRIPTORS OF A PROFICIENT READER | ALWAYS | SOMETIMES | NOT YET |
|---|---|---|---|
| Reads with expression. | | | |
| Stops to self-correct if a word does not make sense. | | | |
| Pays attention to punctuation. | | | |
| Uses phonics skills to sound out new words. | | | |
| Uses context clues to make sense of new words. | | | |
| Skips unknown words, reads on for meaning, then rereads. | | | |
| Understands the passage. | | | |
| Reads silently and correctly answers questions about the passage. | | | |
| | | | |
| | | | |
| | | | |
| | | | |
| | | | |
| | | | |
| | | | |

## Activity Suggestion

Teach your students the attributes of a proficient reader. Ask them to write self-assessments based on the rubric. Then have them choose one skill area at a time to focus on improving.

 # Is This Text Appropriate?

Use this checklist with any passage (or book) to determine if it is the appropriate reading level for a student.

Make two copies of a reading passage. Ask the student to read from one copy of the article while you record on the other.

As the student reads, circle words with which the student has trouble. If the student self-corrects, underline the word.

After the student has read the article, assist her in completing the comprehension activity. Record your observations here.

Student name: _____    Date: _____

Title: _____    Page(s): _____

Reading passage: _____

**Did the student read with expression?**
☐ yes    ☐ no

**List any words with which the student had trouble.**

_____

_____

*If the student had trouble with comprehension or with more than five words in a 50-word passage, the text may be too difficult.*

**Assessment for further instruction:**

_____

**Did the student self-correct?**
☐ yes    ☐ no

**What strategies did the student employ?** (Check all that apply.)
☐ phonics
☐ picture clues
☐ context clues
☐ context plus beginning sound
☐ substitution of a similar word

**Did the student stop reading and go back when meaning was lost?**
☐ yes    ☐ no

**What reading skills are mastered?**
(Check all that apply.)
☐ phonics
☐ picture clues
☐ context clues
☐ context plus beginning sound
☐ substitution of a similar word
☐ fluency

List type(s) of comprehension:

_____

_____

**What specific skill instruction does the student need?**

_____

_____

_____

Name _____

 # Student Reading List

**Write the title of each book you read. Then write about the book.**

Book Title: _____

Author: _____  Genre: _____

What did you like best about the book?

_____

What is the book about?

_____

Write one question you have about the book.

_____

Do you think other people should read this book?   ☐ yes   ☐ no

Book Title: _____

Author: _____  Genre: _____

What did you like best about the book?

_____

What is the book about?

_____

Write one question you have about the book.

_____

Do you think other people should read this book?   ☐ yes   ☐ no

Book Title: _____

Author: _____  Genre: _____

What did you like best about the book?

_____

What is the book about?

_____

Write one question you have about the book.

_____

Do you think other people should read this book?   ☐ yes   ☐ no

## p. 5: Science Experiment
A. It is difficult.
B. air pressure
C. *Pictures will vary.*

## p. 8: What Is the Problem?
1. a. Robbie and his dad
   b. morning, on a beach
   c. A beached whale may die.
   d. *Answers will vary—Biologists may come and rescue the whale.*
2. a. Marjie and Danielle
   b. outside Danielle's house
   c. Marjie's bike is broken.
   d. *Answers will vary—Danielle will apologize and get the bike fixed.*

## p. 9: Easy Dessert
*Pictures will vary but should show the steps in this order:*

1. *Melt butter.*
2. *Pat graham crackers.*
3. *Sprinkle nuts, chocolate chips, and then coconut flakes.*
4. *Pour milk over top and bake.*

## p. 10: Forest Animals

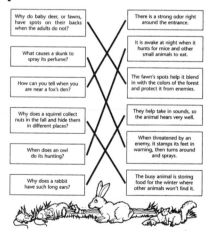

## p. 11: A Scary Story
1. who
2. what
3. where
4. why
5. when

*Stories will vary.*

## p. 13: Home Alone
*Answers will vary.*

## p. 14: What's the Question?
*Some answers may vary.*

1. What are the names of three fairy-tale princesses?
2. What things do you take along on a camping trip?
3. What are four green vegetables?
4. Who was George Washington?
5. Who was Rosa Parks?
6. What is Antarctica?
7. How do you make hot cocoa?
8. What is an insect?

## p. 15: One More Chapter?
| | | |
|---|---|---|
| 1. no | 4. yes | 7. yes |
| 2. yes | 5. no | 8. no |
| 3. no | 6. yes | 9. yes |

*Pictures will vary.*

## p. 17: Saguaro Cactus

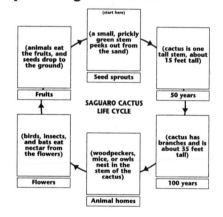

## p. 19: Skateboard
1. Justin gets to pick out each part of the skateboard himself.
2. The deck is the board, or the part where the skater stands.
3. Traction keeps the skater's feet from slipping during tricks.
4. ollie, drop in, rock 'n' roll
5. kick flip, finger flip, board sliding, 50-50 grind

6. quarter pipe, fun box
7. by practicing, watching others, and learning from his brother

*Skateboard designs will vary.*

## p. 20: What Have You Read?
1. 12
2. 9
3. 21
4. Trey, Brendan, Evelyn, and Phillip
5. 10
6. Polly, Jay, Kelly, John, and Ritu

## p. 21: Helen Keller
1. learned to speak with her hands, learned to speak with her voice, went to college, wrote books, taught others, worked against unfairness
2. *Answers will vary. Example: It was hard for Helen to learn to use her voice because she couldn't hear herself.*
3. *Answers will vary but may include strong, smart, dedicated, and famous.*
4. *Answers will vary.*

## p. 23: Compost Pile
*Details may vary.*

1. Not everything you throw away is trash.
   a. Some things can be recycled.
   b. Some things can be burned.
   c. Some things can be composted.
2. A compost pile is simple to make.
   a. You can use a box or a special bin.
   b. You put in shredded newspaper, grass, and leaves.
   c. You can put in food garbage.

## p. 23: Compost Pile (cont.)

3. You have to take care of your compost pile.
   a. You have to stir it.
   b. You have to allow the sun to reach it.
   c. You should water it lightly.
4. A compost pile helps you.
   a. You throw away less garbage.
   b. There is less garbage in the dump.
   c. You pay less for garbage collection.
   d. Compost makes a great fertilizer.
   e. A compost pile is a fun science experiment.

## p. 25: Whales

*Answers may vary.*

## p. 29: Dinosaurs

1. fantasy
2. fact
3. fact
4. fantasy
5. fantasy
6. fantasy
7. fact

*Pictures will vary.*

## p. 31: Lemonade Stand

4 They carried out the heavy cooler.
2 Emily set up the chairs.
8 The neighbor bought some lemonade.
1 The girls set up the table.
6 They put 10 cookies on a plate.
5 They put one pitcher of lemonade on the table.
9 The girls stayed at the lemonade stand for two hours.
10 They earned six dollars.
3 They painted the sign.
7 Two cars drove by without stopping.

*Advertisements will vary.*

## p. 35: Marc Brown

1. He loves to draw and write.
2. He loved her. She was very supportive.
3. He loves them.
4. *Answers will vary.*

A. funny, creative
B. Imagine how exciting it is to use a pencil or computer and your imagination to create whole new worlds and new ideas.

## p. 37: Paper Towels

"I'm sorry to tell you, Mr. Scott, that we have an incorrect shipment of paper from the paper mill."
~~"The paper is bad."~~
"This paper is thick and wrinkled."
"Tissue paper is thin and smooth."
~~"This paper is too tough."~~
~~"Wrinkled paper is ugly!"~~
"This is thick enough to be a hand towel."
~~"Hand towels should be washable."~~

*Answers will vary.*

1. a guitar
2. a hat
3. a picture frame
4. a scooter

## p. 39: Penny's New Glasses

1. Penny could not read the board in class.
2. She turned dials to find the right strength.
3. An optometrist finds the right strength for glasses.
4. An optician helps pick out frames and makes sure the frames and glasses fit.
5. Yes, Penny liked to wear her new glasses.
6. Penny was surprised.
7. She could read math problems on the board, she had no trouble reading books, and she made a basket in gym class.
8. She told a joke.

*Pictures will vary.*

## p. 41: Peterson's Pockets

*Stories will vary.*

## p. 43: Recycling

1. empty soup can – B
   glass soda bottle – A
   mayonnaise jar – A
   used facial tissue – F
   newspaper – C
   cottage cheese container – E
   envelopes – C
   junk mail – C
   pop can – B
   shampoo bottle – E
   crushed box – D
   broken toy – F

2. 

| glass bottles | processed and made into new material |
| broken toys | melted and made into new material |
| junk mail | crushed, melted, and made into new material |
| pop cans | thrown in a garbage dump |

3. Garbage dumps won't fill as quickly. You will use fewer new materials.

4, 5. *Answers will vary.*

## p. 45: Shortcut

1. They took a shortcut home along the railroad tracks.
2. They took a risk.
3. They didn't know when there would be a train.
4. Yes, they had talked about it.
5. They were upset.
6. No, it was too scary and dangerous.
7. They were just glad they weren't hurt worse.

## pp. 46–47: The Doll Store

*Answers will vary.*

## p. 49: The Fort

1. The children lose their fort.
2. They are afraid to ask if they can play there.
3. The neighborhood kids stay away from the fort.
4. Alex and Brian agreed to ask if they could play in the fort.
5. Mrs. Johnson answers the door and they ask her if they can play there.

# Answer Key (continued)

**p. 49: The Fort** (cont.)
6. The children must play safely and quietly.
7. The Johnson kids join them.
8. *Answers will vary.*

**p. 51: What's in an Egg?**

| ANIMAL | DESCRIPTION OF EGG | LOCATION OF EGG |
| --- | --- | --- |
| fish | soft-shelled | water |
| seahorses | soft-shelled | dad's belly pouch |
| octopuses | soft-shelled | hanging in cave |
| oysters | 100,000,000 | water |
| frogs | in clumps | water |
| toads | in long strands | water |
| birds | hard shell | nests |
| penguin | hard shell | father's feet |
| insects | small, in a sac | leaf or branch |
| spiders | wrapped in silk | carried / in a safe place |

**p. 53: A Day at the Beach**
*Answers may vary.*

1. She would have taught Erika how to swim.
2. She was worried that Yesenia would laugh at her.
3. She hadn't spent much time near water.
4. She can spend more time around the water.
5. They played in the waves, made a sand castle, and took a ride in the paddle boat.
6. Yes. They are good friends.
7. Yes. She had a lot of fun.

A. quiet, cautious, a worrier, nervous
B. helpful, brave, caring, kind, a good friend

**p. 54: Columbus Day**

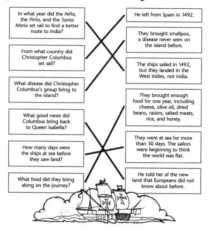

In what year did the *Niña*, the *Pinta*, and the *Santa Maria* set sail to find a better route to India?

He left from Spain in 1492.

From what country did Christopher Columbus set sail?

They brought smallpox, a disease never seen on the island before.

What disease did Christopher Columbus's group bring to the island?

The ships sailed in 1492, but they landed in the West Indies, not India.

What good news did Columbus bring back to Queen Isabella?

They brought enough food for one year, including cheese, olive oil, dried beans, raisins, salted meats, rice, and honey.

How many days were the ships at sea before they saw land?

They were at sea for more than 30 days. The sailors were beginning to think the world was flat.

What food did they bring along on the journey?

He told her of the new land that Europeans did not know about before.

**p. 55: Campfire Walking Salad**
*Pictures will vary but should show the steps in this order:*

1. *Wash the lettuce.*
2. *Spread mayonnaise or peanut butter on the lettuce.*
3. *Add other ingredients.*
4. *Roll up and eat.*

**p. 57: A Family Hike**
1. No, it is a family event.
2. a teenager
3. No, but it is probably a girl.
4. yes
   "It was a wonderful morning."
   "I love this place!"
5. in the mountains
6. summer
7. Yes, they know all about hiking and have lots of gear.
8. sight, hearing, and smell
   *Examples will vary.*

Don't rush.
Getting there is half the fun.
Listen, did you hear that?
Take one step at a time.

**p. 58: Animal Diagram**
1. All the animals have spots.
2. All the animals are in the cat family.
3, 4. *Answers will vary.*

**p. 59: Advertisement**
1. a Snuggle Pet
2. Everyone should have one.
3. It can do tricks, you don't have to feed or bathe it, it snuggles with you, and it comes in a variety of animals.
4. nothing
5. extra costs, some assembly required

**p. 61: Chewing Gum**
1. curious
2. proud
3. replace rubber
4. He was silly.

A. He "invented" chewing gum.
B, C. *Summaries will vary.*

**p. 63: Don't Bug Me!**
1. female
2. blood, eggs
3. eat
4. human
5. lay her eggs
6. clot
7. proboscis
8. chemical
9. itchy
10. swelling, turning red, and getting itchy
11. whine
12. bug spray

*Poems will vary.*

# Answer Key (continued)

## p. 65: Insects
1. Insects are interesting.
2. Insects' sense organs are in different parts of the body than in humans.
3. Insects can be helpful.
4. Insects can be harmful.
5. Insects make the world more interesting.

*Pictures will vary.*

## p. 67: Managing Fires
1. A firefighter should be brave, know how to use a hose and an axe, and be able to act and think quickly.
2. A fire should be left to burn if it is started by lightning and if it won't hurt people.
3. A controlled fire is contained by firefighters. It will not spread to where it may hurt people or property.
4. It helps to burn up the fuel needed by the forest fire.
5. Being brave means facing danger.
6. He watches to make sure the fire does not burn out of control.
7. It can burn messy downed trees and make room for new growth.
8. Being careless means not thinking about the consequences of your actions.

## p. 69: Paul Bunyan
1. He cut five trees with one swing, wrestled with bears, dug the St. Lawrence Seaway, carved the Grand Canyon, and cleared the Great Plains.
2, 3. *Answers will vary.*

## p. 71: The Giant Sequoia
1. millions of years
2. 500 years
3. 83 meters (274 feet) tall
4. more than 3,000 years
5. It clears the underbrush and opens the cones to release seeds.
6. They need warmth. People trample the ground near their roots.
7. They absorb water through their roots.
8. They need water and warmth.
9. It creates animal homes and fertilizer.

## p. 73: Taking Care of Teeth
1. to teach
2. a factual article
3. the history of dental care

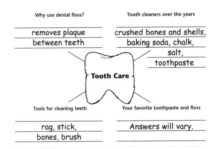

| Why use dental floss? | Tooth cleaners over the years |
| --- | --- |
| removes plaque between teeth | crushed bones and shells, baking soda, chalk, salt, toothpaste |

**Tooth Care**

| Tools for cleaning teeth | Your favorite toothpaste and floss |
| --- | --- |
| rag, stick, bones, brush | Answers will vary. |

## p. 75: The Zoo
1. the baby-sitter
2. 12 to 15 years old—old enough to baby-sit but too young to drive
3. four and one
4. Will
5. no
6. yes / "I like to baby-sit for my little cousins."
7. They watched the monkeys, ate lunch, went to the gift shop, and played on the playground.
8. summer / it's hot and the kids are not in school on a Thursday

## p. 77: Limericks
*Poems will vary.*

## p. 78: Nonsense Words
1. park        4. crack
2. pet         5. stick
3. rock        6. watch

## p. 79: Ellie and Polly
1. no     4. no     7. yes
2. yes    5. no     8. no
3. yes    6. no     9. yes

*Pictures should show a girl and a dog walking to an ice cream shop.*

## p. 81: Making Money
1. Rob, his mom and dad, neighbors, and Rob's friends
2. Rob
3. Rob Kolbe is hard-working and determined.
4. Rob needs money for a school trip to Washington, D.C.
5. He will work to earn half of the money if his parents can provide the other half.
6. He baby-sits, does yard work, and delivers papers.
7. yes
8. proud
9. *Answers will vary.*

## p. 83: Mermaid or Sea Cow?

Manatees inspired the sailors' stories of mermaids.

Manatees make high-pitched sounds.

~~Manatees are big and ugly.~~

~~Manatees make a horrible noise.~~

Manatees are mammals that breathe air.

They live in shallow waters.

~~Boats are more important than animals.~~

Manatees eat grasses underwater.

Their only enemy is people.

~~Hunting is bad.~~

Hunting manatees is against the law.

~~It is okay for the manatee to become extinct.~~

Boat propellers can hurt manatees.

~~Shallow waters should be used just by people for swimming and boating.~~

Signs tell people about where manatees live so people can watch out for them.

~~Children should pick up trash.~~

~~Manatees are interesting animals.~~

## p. 87: Plastic

| | |
|---|---|
| 1. opinion | 7. fact |
| 2. fact | 8. opinion |
| 3. opinion | 9. opinion |
| 4. opinion | 10. opinion |
| 5. fact | 11. opinion |
| 6. opinion | |

*Pictures will vary.*

## p. 89: Publishing a Book

**6** Editor helps author rewrite the story.
**1** Author gets an idea.
**10** The printer and binder put the book together.
**5** Editor offers to publish the story.
**9** Artist draws pictures.
**7** Editor plans the book with the designer.
**2** Author writes a story.
**8** Designer hires an artist.
**4** Author sends the story to an editor.
**11** The books are shipped all over the world.
**3** Author makes all the words just right.
**12** You buy the book in a bookstore.

*Answers will vary.*

## p. 91: Sharks

| | |
|---|---|
| 1. false | 8. true |
| 2. true | 9. false |
| 3. false | 10. false |
| 4. false | 11. true |
| 5. true | 12. false |
| 6. true | 13. true |
| 7. true | 14. false |

## p. 93: Sod Houses

First paragraph
Main idea: Pioneers made temporary houses.
Details: busy planting gardens and crops, digging wells, preparing for winter

Second paragraph
Main idea: The pioneers made sod houses.
Details: not many trees around, tough sod was thick with roots, cut top layer of soil into bricks, roots helped cement bricks together

Third paragraph
Main idea: The well-made soddy was comfortable and dry.
Details: wooden frames and glass for doors and windows, roofs of straw and dirt or wood and sod, stayed cool in summer and warm in winter

Fourth paragraph
Main idea: Animals lived with the pioneers in the soddy.
Details: snakes, insects, mice, and dirt

Fifth paragraph
Main idea: Pioneers were strong, determined people.
Details: worked hard, clever use of natural resources

## p. 95: The *Mayflower*

1. The journey was dangerous. They did a lot of hard work. They were away from home.
2. They loved the job, and it paid good money.
3. They were looking for freedom and wanted their own land.
4. They had to stay below deck and often became seasick. It was also hard to cook and do other things.
5. They would have been in the way.
6. They had to clean and keep the ship in good shape.
7. Food: They had to cook their own food. Today, ships serve fancy meals.
   Sleeping: They had to sleep together in a big room. Today, ships have private cabins.
   Fresh air: They had to stay below deck and had no fresh air. Today, you can walk around on deck.
   How the ship was powered: They had to use sails. Today, they use motors.
8. They will have to build homes from scratch and grow their own food. There are no stores, and winter is coming.

## p. 97: The *Titanic*

1. In first class, passengers could choose from a menu. In second class, passengers were served a set four-course meal.
2. First-class cabins had sitting rooms.
3. In first and second class, the passengers all had cabins. In third class, some families had cabins, but most passengers slept together in large rooms—one for men and one for women.
4. This was a special trip on the finest ship ever built.

**1** "I love my room. I have a beautiful bedroom with a private sitting room."
**2** "My favorite meal is dinner when we have a delicious four-course meal."
**1** "We swam for hours in the pool."
**3** "In the evening, we sit on benches in the only room we all share. We play music and dance."
**2** "I love to sit on the deck in the sun. My brother likes to play under the lifeboats."
**3** "We had a nice meal. We had to eat a little fast so the next group of people could come in and eat."

## p. 99: Tipi

1. They followed the buffalo.
2. They needed portable homes.
3. The buffalo were hunted until they became scarce.
4. They would poke holes in the tipi cover.
5. They wore out and had to be replaced.
6. It softened the hides.
7. It cured the hides to make them last longer and prevent them from cracking.
8. They blocked out the west wind and could see the rising sun in the morning.

# Answer Key (continued)

**p. 99: Tipi (cont.)**
9. Hunting and westward expansion led to the creation of reservations.
10. *Answers will vary.*

**p. 101: Wolves**
*Answers will vary.*

| Negative Characteristics | Positive Characteristics |
|---|---|
| • eat small animals | • shy |
| • eat ranchers' animals | • only attack people when threatened |
| • good hunters | • keep populations down |
| • sharp teeth | • hunt weak and sickly |

*Fairy tales will vary.*

**p. 103: Yellowstone Fires**
1. It clears the brush, opens meadows, starts new growth, and makes new homes for animals.
2. dry weather and lightning
3. ground is covered with dead trees, no new growth, no meadows
4. everything was dry, dead trees on the ground ignited
5. heat from the fires
6. new growth provided food and homes, new meadows
7. Another fire will be needed to control the growth.
8. positive—*Explanations will vary.*
9. too much growth, fallen trees
10. snowfall

**pp. 104–105: Listening to Music**
*Answers will vary.*

**p. 107: Ty Cobb**
1. He got into fights, sharpened his cleats, and intimidated others.
2. He was a great hitter.
3. It meant that he was the best.
4. His nickname was the "Georgia Peach."

*Charts will vary but should include statistics mentioned in the text.*

**p. 109: Scientific Classification**
1. They belong to the same kingdom, phylum, and subphylum but to different classes, orders, and species.
2.

**Kingdoms**

Moneran (M)　Protist (Pr)　Fungi (F)　Plant (Pl)　Animal (A)

**Pl** yellow rose　**Pl** oak tree　**M** single-celled blue-green algae
**A** starfish　**A** human　**F** portabella mushroom
**A** ostrich　**A** centipede　**Pr** single-celled amoeba (with nucleus)

3, 4. *Answers will vary.*

**p. 111: Sailing in a Storm**
1. Yes. She says they "loved to go sailing together."
2. They were disappointed. They had wanted to shop and eat in town.
3. They would rather have used the sails.
4. They turned off the motor and sailed.
5. One person had to take down the sails while the other steered the boat. Tina chose to steer.
6. They were thinking about the trip.
7. She felt safe there.
8, 9. *Answers will vary.*
10. She was shivering with fear.

**p. 113: John Adams**
1. He was so dedicated to the independence movement that he was rarely home.
2. *Answers will vary.*
3. He helped create the Declaration of Independence. He served as President of the United States for four years.

**p. 116: Questions and Answers**

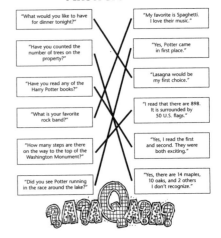

**pp. 117–119: Comprehension Review Test**
1. winter
2. Santa
3. presents
4. bringing gifts
5. Maddie is too busy.
6. the car
7. don't do her homework
8. flying to other planets
9. space station
10. They both have lungs.
11. The dolphin's snout is more pointed.
12. Emily doesn't know what to do with her dollhouse.
13. a bear
14. watching the sunset
15. outside
16. in a tree
17. plucked his whiskers